Tearing Down Walls

Ich Bin Ein Berliner

An autobiographical novel

Volume II

Lawrence H. Staples, Ph.D.

 CHIRON PUBLICATIONS • ASHEVILLE, NORTH CAROLINA

© 2022 by Chiron Publications. All rights reserved. No part of this publication may be reproduced, stored in a retrieval system, or transmitted, in any form by any means, electronic, mechanical, photocopying, recording, or otherwise, without the prior written permission of the publisher, Chiron Publications, P.O. Box 19690, Asheville, N.C. 28815-1690.

www.ChironPublications.com

Interior and cover design by Danijela Mijailovic
Printed primarily in the United States of America.

ISBN 978-1-68503-064-3 paperback
ISBN 978-1-68503-065-0 hardcover
ISBN 978-1-68503-066-7 electronic
ISBN 978-1-68503-067-4 limited edition paperback

Library of Congress Cataloging-in-Publication Data Pending

DEDICATED TO MY MOTHER,
AILEEN SUE BURNETT,
AND MY GRANDMOTHER,
ALICE ELISABETH STAPLES

Before I built a wall I'd ask to know
What I was walling in or walling out,
And to whom I was like to give offense.
Something there is that doesn't love a wall,
That wants it down.

- Robert Frost
"Mending Wall"

PREFACE

Like Berlin, we all have a wall that needs to be torn down. It's a wall we built at a young age, when socialization began, and we needed a barrier behind which we could hide that part of ourselves that was unacceptable to our mothers and others who guided our development. As in the case of Berlin, the wall keeps us from becoming all we can be. Berlin, thus, is a metaphor for the enlargement of personality that can occur when we, like Berlin's inhabitants, tear down that wall and become bigger, richer, freer, and more diverse and democratic. In this sense, we are all potentially Berliners.

Most people my age remember Berlin before the wall. They remember when the wall was built and when it was torn down. They remember President Reagan in Berlin in 1990 saying, "Mr. Gorbachev, tear down this wall." Soon, the Berlin wall did come down. And anyone who visits Berlin today will see for himself how that produced the resplendent, creative miracle the city has become.

Today, however, there is still another wall. This one is uniquely American, and it threatens our collective self the way the Berlin wall threatened Berliners. East and West are replaced by Democratic and Republican. We see each other as enemies. We are suspicious of each other. Even essential collaboration that would help both sides is difficult, if not impossible. Like the divided Berlin before its wall came down, we've lost the strength that comes from unity.

East Berliners and West Berliners found the synergistic power of union only after they realized they were Berliners, not East or West, but of the city as a whole. We have to see, as Berliners finally did, that when East fights West, each fights itself. When Democrat fights Republican, they fight themselves. With division, we become blinded to how desperately we need each other. If we look inside ourselves, we see that we are Americans, just as East and West Berliners saw they were Berliners. It's a bigger, more potent definition of ourselves.

I am you; you are me; together we are one. When we see ourselves this way, a creative process is unleashed, and we become who we totally are. We find we are greater than the sum of our parts. We find that there is much more to us than we ever imagined, just as Berliners did when they joined together as one.

But tearing down the wall isn't all the work; it's the beginning of the work. Much remains to be done once the wall is down. Like East Berlin, that side of our wall is undeveloped. It needs attention; it needs huge investments of time and energy; it needs to be brought into the light and illuminated so that we can see it fully and understand its potential to enrich and fulfill our lives.

Jung once wrote that, "As any change must begin somewhere, it is the single individual who will undergo it and carry it through. The change must begin with one individual..." (Jung, 1953/1973, para. 599). In other words, if you want to change the world, you must change yourself rather than trying to change others. Tearing down one's interior wall is such a change.

This book is about important parts of the process I followed in order to tear down my wall, expose the shadow behind it and, thereby, contribute my tiny portion to the achievement of a collective need.

Berlin is a metaphor for what I can become, what we all can become, if we can tear down our walls.

· · · · · · · · · · ·

ACKNOWLEDGMENTS

I want to thank my wife, Nancy Pennington, for her enduring love and support, which continues despite her knowledge of the darker side of myself and the outrageous, pathetic, childish, and selfish behaviors that lie there. She also helped me in many ways with the preparation of the manuscript of this book. Her laser-like insights, which can go quickly and directly to the heart of things, were especially appreciated.

Karen Farley, who has edited several books for me and my wife, put her deft hand and amazing literacy to work on this one. Thanks, Karen. Your gifts often feel magical and always add clarity and precision to our work.

I also want to thank Dr. Enrico Buratti, of Florence, Italy, a friend and colleague whose keen insights and creative interpretations helped me more fully understand the meaning and import of the dream that led to this book.

A BIG DREAM

The creative catalyst for this book was a numinously powerful dream: In the dream, it is very late at night or early in the morning, and I am in a small, isolated farmhouse. The house looks as though it is made of rough, unpainted cedar. A few steps lead up to a small front porch. The house is not in good condition. I hear a knock at the door, open it, and see Jesus standing on the front porch in an old, knee-length robe, a tattered rope tied around his waist. I ask him who he is. Jesus replies, "*Ich bin ein Berliner.*"

The dream touched me deeply. I wondered what it could mean.

Most of us who are old enough will never forget those famous words spoken by President Kennedy during his visit to Berlin in 1963. We can remember the reason for his visit. Berlin at that time was like an island surrounded by hostile Russian forces. Kennedy's speech was a declaration of support to Berliners who felt threatened and afraid. The moment "*Ich bin ein Berliner*" escaped his lips, the crowd erupted. They could feel the meaning. They were no longer alone. America was with them. It was as if they had felt saved by a power greater than themselves.

My dream had come at a time of considerable stress and despair in my life. Like the Berliners of those days, I felt threatened and afraid. My health, finances, relationships, and well-being were in perilous shape. The dream, like Kennedy's words to Berliners, comforted me. I too felt saved by a power greater than myself.

In the years since having this dream, I have spent much time and effort trying to interpret and understand it. While I may never fully comprehend it, I feel sure it has an important meaning for me.

Over time, I came to believe that Jesus was an image of the Self, and I began to wonder what it meant for the Self to be a Berliner. One way I have come to think about what it means for the Self to be a Berliner is to imagine that Berlin is a symbol of and a metaphor for the Creator, and, as such, a reflection of those mysterious creative processes that grow and build and change things until they become what they are meant to be. It is a beautiful symbol of teleological unfolding that led Berlin to what it is today and led me to what I am. Let us remember that a metaphor of a thing is not the thing; it is a representation of the thing.

Berlin has grown from a pile of rubble after World War II to a stunning creative entity extremely diverse in its makeup, containing the opposites, the contradictions, and the paradoxes found in all creations. On the surface, Berlin is orderly and structured. But deep underneath is a teeming, chaotic, perhaps, even Dionysian layer that bursts with life. Two recent television series, *Babylon Berlin* and *Oktoberfest*, provide a glimpse into this contrast. It's as if the finger of God touched this chaotic layer below and produced the incredible manifest beauty that is the Berlin we see today.

For me personally, to be a Berliner refers to the creative developmental process that developed me and other humans just as it developed Berlin. It's about starting out as a unified whole, as we all started out as infants, as Berlin itself started out. It is then to be split in two with a wall erected between the two parts, as Berlin was, and as we all were when socialization began, shattering our original wholeness. Finally, it is to become one again, as Berlin has done and as we hope to do in our individual and collective lives, if we do our work and if we are lucky. In many ways, I suspect I have felt about my inner wall the way Berliners felt about theirs. There is a deep yearning to tear it down.

The first time I was in Berlin was 1958. Still visible was much of the aftermath of World War II. All around one still saw the skeletal remains of bombed-out buildings and vacant spaces. I spent the night in a hotel whose roof had not yet been fully repaired. I could actually see the sky and stars through the ceiling as I lay in bed. Other parts of the roof were covered with canvas. A few years later, the wall was built so that Berlin was divided not only politically but also physically.

I doubt anyone seeing the divided, war-devastated Berlin of those days could fully imagine the Berlin of today. The wall is torn down. The city is once again united. It is as if some tiny spark smoldering in the ashes left by the war flickered and then caught, blazing up and generating the heat, the light, the energy, and the passion needed to transform it into the stunningly beautiful and thriving city it is today: its eclectic architecture, its monuments, concert halls, churches, and tree-lined avenues. Berlin has grown into *ein grelles licht*, or "a bright light," attracting artists, scientists, and intellectuals, a rich and diverse mix of people representing many religions, nationalities, and races. Compared to the city I saw many years ago, the Berlin of today is a picture of almost miraculous transformation. In the end, I have concluded that to be a Berliner is to be the result of a creative process that unfolds us, as it did Berlin, into who we are, that unfolds everything else into what it is.

It is important to be mindful that we can never accurately say or describe who we are. Since we are ever-changing, as Berlin is, we can only accurately describe ourselves as a process. It is not difficult to imagine that that process survives the shedding of our mortal coil and continues into eternity. This suggests that we actually never achieve full unity. We are, however, ever moving toward it. Though I use the words "ever-changing" to describe the process, there is also something unchanging about it. The words "ever-changing" capture the idea of permanence. At one level we are constantly changing, and at another we are remaining the same. That is probably why we both know ourselves to be who we were when we were children but also who we are many years later, after a lifetime of changes. It's also why we can never put our finger on who we truly are. Cezanne was clearly aware of this process of change when he would paint the same landscape at different times on succeeding days. The way the landscape opened out through this series of paintings holds within it the idea that creation is a process, that Cezanne's efforts would have had to continue into eternity in order to fully capture the scene in all its facets and perspectives. We could also look at his paintings and see his original painting in his hundredth one, despite all the intervening changes. Of course, I could say the same about this book. It can never truly be fully finished. It would keep changing too, if I could keep at it. But some of it would remain the same. In truth, we'll never really know who we are; we'll only get snapshots. The problem is that we are moving pictures. We are the same person we were at the beginning of the movie, but we are also more than that.

If Jesus is a Berliner, then he is very different from the biblical description of him. He is much bigger than that. He is not just love and kindness and forgiveness. He, like Berlin, contains infinite diversity, darkness and light, and all the contradictions that comprise creation. So do you. So do I.

Life has taken me through many twists and turns in order for me to know who I am. Berlin went through a similar sinuous process. I think all our lives are, like Berlin, formed by this creative process. It's the cause, and, therefore, the reason for our existence. We serve creation, the Creator's purpose, and we do it whether we like it or not. As Jung once said, "*Mann kann freiwillig gehen oder geschleppt geworden*." We can either go willingly or be dragged.[1] I've always been a

---

[1] I heard this at a lecture at the Jung Institute-Zürich, but I don't remember seeing it in writing.

Berliner. My conscious mind just didn't know it until I started writing this book. The writing knew where it was going and took me there with it. In a sense, my writing was the tow truck that dragged me to its destination.

In a very superficial way, I just thought I had bounced around pretty aimlessly in my life, with one thing leading to another without any particular connectedness, rhyme, or reason. The bouncing led from Ardmore, Oklahoma, to St. Louis, to Cambridge and Boston, to Asheville, to Zürich, to Washington, D.C., to Sanibel Island, Florida, and then back to Ardmore, where I was born. I passed through Thomas Jefferson School, Harvard College, Harvard Business School, a Fortune 500 company, The Jung Institute-Zürich, a private psychoanalytic practice in Washington, D.C., and, finally, on to retirement. I ended up with my body in Ardmore, where I started out, and my soul in Berlin, which was thousands of miles away from my beginning.

As I am thinking about this journey, I am remembering that in Zürich I became fluent in German. That was thirty-five years ago. I didn't have to learn German in order to complete studies at The Jung Institute. I learned German because it served a love interest. I met and fell in love with a Swiss woman who didn't speak English. Believe me, German is a very difficult language to learn at any age, but I was fifty-five. The need for love motivated me to become fluent in German in a few short months. While at the time I thought I was learning German only to connect to this lovely woman, I find myself thinking now that my learning German was preparing me to know I am a Berliner years before I had any idea that that is who I was.

Then, my interests led me from Zürich to Washington, where I met the love of my life. I am pretty sure I believed I had to achieve a lot creatively to hold on to her. I'm not saying she thought that. But the truth is that I never wrote a book until I met her and fell in love. Then, I wrote three books and co-wrote two other books with her. And all along she encouraged me and helped me with my writing. I don't think it is possible to recount all the ways that she helped me write. For one thing, she shared with me invaluable insights that enhanced my writing. She edited and helped with obtaining permissions and a whole host of other things necessary to write books and get them published. She was heavily involved. None of that means she would love me only if I achieved creatively; it just meant that is what I thought and, perhaps, projected onto her. And I have to admit that those projected thoughts were at best subconscious. But I was highly motivated by what I thought, even if my thinking was faulty. I simply can't help wondering if the Creator used my love for her as a way of motivating me to create. I needed love. I thought I had to create in order to get her to love me and to sustain it. Is this the way the Muse works? Does she make you fall in love with her before you can play the lyre? Here I am, five books after meeting her and falling in love.

This is just another more recent example of the magical thinking that comes to me increasingly with growing age. Apparently, as I age my ego gets weaker, and the membrane between it and the unconscious weakens to a point where a lot more primitive feelings and ideas slip through. I thought magically that it was the books that kept her loving me. What I really suspect is that the Creator doesn't care whether I loved her or she loved me, as long as the hope for love kept me creating. The Creator doesn't care about love per se; the Creator just cares about what love can do for creation. Let's face it. Love produces both biological and artistic children. Babies and books are caused by the same thing. They are two different ways of getting pregnant, but one requires actual masculine and feminine intercourse in the outer world and the other spiritual masculine and feminine conjunction in our inner world.

The weakened membrane that allows the more magical and primitive thinking to slip through, may also allow a lurking or even encroaching dementia to make border incursions. Despite my weakened state, I am fortunately able, more or less, to string together sentences that have some semblance of logic, coherence and connectedness. I may be able to escape the worst before darkness falls.

It has been a long trip, a long journey. I am tired but relieved to be what must be close to the end, at least, what seems close to the end. I'm not sure what happens after you find out who you are. A mundane question is, "Do I stay physically in Ardmore, or do I move to Berlin? Does my soul need my body to follow it to Berlin in order to be completely whole, or is the spirit enough?" Up to this point, fate has answered the question. I don't yet have the money that would be necessary to move to Berlin.

The fact that the money necessary to move to Berlin has not materialized causes me to imagine that you don't really have to live in Berlin to be a Berliner. I can imagine that to be a Berliner is a psychological rather than physical state. But I'm not yet certain about that. I'm feeling very restless in Ardmore. I must like to keep on the move. My wife Nancy calls me her "tumbleweed." I just seem to keep getting blown from place to place, or so it seems, unless some kind of unconscious knowingness knows whither the wind bloweth.

Because Berlin itself is a symbol of transformation and the creativity that that implies, being a Berliner means being a creator. We are all creators with a little "c," rather like Santa's helpers are santas with a little "s." For creation to be complete, every little "c" counts, just as every little piece in a jigsaw puzzle counts, if the jigsaw is to be complete. All the little "c's" serve the big "C" in the same way all our little cells serve the body, the same way all the little pieces serve the creation of the complete puzzle. I believe that our creative engines are fueled by feelings, both positive and negative, both constructive and destructive. I had thought my life was fueled by a need for love, but now I think it is fueled by a need for creation, which love and all the other feelings serve.

Everything serves the Creator's purpose, which is creative achievement without end. And I do believe that the need for love is one of the most important feelings that the Creator uses to lead us to creative achievement. For most of our lives there is an insufficiency of what we need. But I think the lifelong discontent we experience from not feeling completely loved, as we felt briefly in infancy, is part of the

Creator's arrangement to keep us creating. We spend our lives trying to do and create the things we think will bring us love, whether it is making good grades or a lot of money, or writing a book, taking care of our siblings, or painting a picture that makes us famous. And on and on.

I can feel some disappointment when I think about my own failure to achieve all that I felt I should achieve, if I were to be fully loved. For most of my life, I felt a dilemma about what I had to do to be loved. The dilemma was caused by a mixed message that I received both from Christianity and my mother. Is it faith or works that brings us love and salvation? The message that ended up dominating my life was that it was not only works, but successful works, that are approved and loved. In the dream, however, it was clear that Jesus, the Self, doesn't come when you are living in a mansion like the ones that I not only fantasize about living in, but believe neurotically will bring me love and admiration. My dream made me realize that Jesus comes when we are poor, living modestly, maybe when we are down and out or have hit bottom, not when we are highly successful. The dream is a kind of fulfillment of the Beatitudes.

The first message we get from mother was also more like the Beatitudes. In infancy we receive from her a look of pure, unconditional love that she gives when she first sees us, as if we were the first sunrise. No matter what happened afterward, we felt looked upon as Jesus was looked upon by the Magi and by Mary. Paradoxically, we felt that love from her even when we were expressing many of the qualities that her frowns later caused us to try to hide from her in order to hold on to her love: dependence, irresponsibility, being dirty or unkempt, being loud, whiny, or complaining, and expressing interest in touching and sucking the most sexually attractive parts of mother, her breasts. But before those frowns, she loved us, and she loved us before we had achieved anything except mere being. So, her first message was also like the Beatitudes. We didn't have to lift a finger to be loved and taken care of. After that, however, socialization began, and we got a new message. "You are only lovable when you are faithful to mother and when you achieve all the things she thinks are worthwhile." We build a psychic wall behind which we try to hide all the things she does not approve of. Mother's post-socialization message — that we have to do what she approves of — leads us to constant lifelong striving to meet her wishes. And it creates constant dissatisfaction because of our helpless tendency to err and be imperfect. We keep striving, hoping that someday we will satisfy her and feel fulfilled.

It is a feeling that, unfortunately, endures even into old age, when we theoretically should be smelling the roses. Look at me. I've just turned ninety, and I still feel that I have not achieved enough. I must still have hope. I continue to try to achieve, even while believing that my achievements thus far have been of little use to mankind, have brought only meager earthly rewards and little of the love that I originally experienced from mother. It's pathetic in a way. My mind knows that if I think I will ever be satisfied I am kidding myself. My mind also suspects that nature wired us that way so that we will keep trying till our last breath. Goethe described this incessant dissatisfaction as "divine discontent"

(1949, p. xiii), a kind of restlessness that drives us to try to achieve things that will reduce the dissatisfaction. This perpetual feeling of dissatisfaction with ourselves has been described as an Imposter Syndrome, a collection of feelings of inadequacy that persist despite evident success. I've suffered this syndrome for much of my life.

But incessant dissatisfaction can also feel as if I want something the Creator, the Self, doesn't want me to have. It can feel as though I am fighting against the Self. I seem to be saying that the Self has wired me, and perhaps all humans, to want more than he will allow. But we Jungians talk about the ego/Self alignment, the need to get the ego's will and God's will to be the same. Somehow, I am having difficulty reconciling the two concepts. I can even think what a relief it would be for me to want exactly what the Self wants for me. Just accepting that could bring a certain peace. Divine discontent leads to just the opposite. Then I think that maybe Goethe was wrong. Or maybe Jung was wrong. I know whose view is winning in my experience, at least on this subject. I am constantly dissatisfied and want more than I have. I know that to be palpably true. I just don't know why. The thought intruded that maybe I should go back to church. There's still a superstition in me that all the answers are found there. That's what spending the first ten years of your life in your grandmother's bed will do for you.

But maybe there is a more simple and forthright reason for why I am obsessed at times with material things, especially houses. When we lived in Asheville, my former wife had a good friend who was the wife of a prominent black doctor. One day my wife was talking with her, and she was lamenting about all the expensive toys her husband, was constantly buying — his convertible Mercedes, his watches, his cameras. Struggling to explain, the doctor's wife, despite her impeccable English, chose the vernacular to dramatize her point: growing up, "he ain't never had nothin." That may be my story, too. And it may be a better explanation of my behavior and fantasies than such highfalutin ideas as divine discontent.

If we think about achievement, success, and recognition in a certain way, the wish to do great things can seem both sad and inflated. Let's take Emmanuel Macron, the president of France. I am sure he and his mother and friends are proud of his great achievements. The truth is, however, that outside of France, and to some extent Europe, his name and accomplishments are almost unknown. What percentage of Americans or Canadians or even Italians, his next-door neighbor, could name who is president of France? I feel pretty sure that the vast majority of us will not be as much as a footnote in history, even if we write good books, or become professors at major universities or well known in our fields. Only a small percentage of the world will recognize us even if we accomplished things that family, friends, and neighbors thought were laudatory, as they must have in Macron's case. In this sense, we are really pretty insignificant despite our wishes to be otherwise. Still, the creative puzzle is incomplete without our sometimes seemingly pitiful contributions. And, despite the likelihood of a relatively insignificant fate, we, I, keep behaving, for the most part futilely, as if widely recognized fame and fortune are still possible, if we just try hard enough.

There is still another view worth stating that can actually make us feel helpless in our drive for accomplishment. It takes will power to accomplish things. But how much of our will power do we control? Jung stated (1954/1974) that, "I regard the will as the amount of psychic energy at the disposal of consciousness" (para. 844), which I interpret as meaning that will power is the amount of psychic energy the Self makes available to the conscious ego, that the ego has the necessary will power to accomplish something only when the Self agrees with what the ego wishes. I can still feel subjectively, even in my old age, that I have will power and can achieve a lot of things I want to achieve. But my mind knows from painful experiences — like trying to diet, trying to stop drinking, trying to refrain from dangerous sex, and so on, that my will power can fail or be withdrawn at any moment without any advance notice. It is then, if we are self-reflective, that we realize that the will power never belonged to us and was never subject to our control. I have wondered if the purpose of addiction, and the loss of control that goes with it, is to humble us so that we are periodically reminded we are not the Self.

All this has led me to the late-life conclusion that I have achieved and will achieve all that, and only that, which the Self wants me to achieve, no more and no less. I can either like it or lump it, as they say. It's pretty humbling, and I tend to lump it more than like it, all the while suspecting the Self is having a good laugh. On the other hand, the humility we gain from our inability to achieve all we want to achieve may make us less critical and judgmental of others and, thus, greatly improve our relationships with them.

In my case, my great need to be successful manifested itself in a number of ways. First, I actually did want solid accomplishments to give evidence of my success. Possibly of equal importance was to appear successful. After all, as my mother often said, what is the point of doing something well and worthwhile if other family members, friends, and neighbors don't see it or know about it? She was definitely in the "don't hide your light under a bushel basket" school. It was a lifelong valuation that made appearances very important to me, despite a conscious wish not to be so shallow. But I also wasn't a dummy. Some part of me knew that to be considered successful in life, we have to appear to be successful and to hide many things that might suggest otherwise. What we hide is what we call the "shadow." To conceal it, we create a wall that we call the "persona."

"Persona" is a Jungian term for the face we show to the world, that is, the process of deciding what we reveal and what we don't, our capacity and inclination to hide the things about us that we don't want others to see. Voicing one's confessions is, of course, the exact opposite of presenting a carefully crafted persona to the world, so much so that I can't help thinking that, had I written this book before I began to practice, I might have had no clients. I probably also would have had fewer friends, admiring colleagues, or others who might otherwise have admired me. Even now the very idea of others reading this book makes me nervous, probably for the same reason that the thought of someone reading my journals once made me equally nervous. Journals tend to reflect a partial picture of a person, often quite unflattering and containing truths that one normally doesn't wish to publicly display. I can say the same about this book. If you read it, you will likely understand why I was reluctant to offer it for publication. In it, I reveal many of my trespasses, and expose for all to view a part, and I really mean just a part, of the dark side of my two-sided moon.

I've known instinctively that, as long as success in the outer world remained an important goal, it was unwise to reveal some of these less flattering aspects of myself. In the second half of life, and even more so in late life, when success in the inner world begins to take precedence, such revelations can be therapeutic, despite their potential to disappoint many who have known us less fully. I'm hoping that my revelations may not only encourage others to take this therapeutic step but also give them the comfort of knowing that they aren't alone in the darker sides of themselves and in the secrets they may harbor. At my age, I feel like all I reveal in this book has been like a cleansing bath. In some ways, it feels therapeutic. As we grow older, I suspect we could all benefit from doing what Proust did: writing a full confession of our lives, even if we can't write as beautifully or deeply as he did. And if we do reveal ourselves this fully and someone still loves us, we may for the first time in our lives truly believe it.

Fortunately, we learn in our psychoanalytic training the importance of presenting to our patients as blank a slate as we can. In order to honor this principle, I remained as best

I could a "tabla rasa" throughout my professional career as an analyst. I believe the mysterious, highly creative processes of the transference work best under those conditions. This level of anonymity led me to believe I was not the one actually producing the therapeutic work of analysis, just as I don't believe I was the one actually writing my books. It's the creative process that does the work, and we are merely the conduits for that process. At least, whether I am right or wrong in that belief, that's the way it feels to me. I remember a training analyst in Zürich telling us that anytime we begin to pat ourselves on the back for our wonderful work and results, we can retain some necessary humility if we imagine that there is a mirror sitting on our left shoulder, that the patient is actually talking with it, and that the mirror is doing the real work.

I'm thankful that I presented a blank enough slate to clients that I could have a rich and meaningful experience as an analyst and could meet and get to know so many fine and interesting people. I also think I helped most of the people who came to me for analysis. For much of my life, I wisely did a pretty good job of concealing large parts of myself not only from clients, but also from colleagues and others I knew. While at my advanced age I feel safer revealing more of myself, I am not without anxiety as I begin this lengthy confession that exposes long-concealed parts of myself. For one thing, I have worried about what my revelations might do to the good image of Jungian analysis. Upon reflection, I have to dismiss the vain and inflated thought that I am important enough or known well enough to have any effect whatsoever. Actually,

I worry more about what it would do to my psyche and soul if I didn't expose myself more fully. I ask myself how anyone can feel genuinely loved and respected if he only allows the bright side of his moon to be seen. It seems to me one would feel only partially loved. I will say, if anyone loves and respects me after reading what I am about to unload, I would probably believe them. I know that life can be very cruel to those who dare public honesty. There are too many famous examples of those who dared for me to enumerate here. But life can feel meaningless, empty, and lonely to those who don't dare to reveal themselves. We suffer either way, but at least we can choose the way in which we suffer.

Nevertheless, despite my frequent disdain, even revulsion, for my shallow persona, a kind of wall that hides my darker side, I believe that without that wall the first half of life would have been devoid of even a modicum of the outer success I needed and craved, just as the second half of life would have lacked the inner success, the richness and realness that the shadow brings, if the wall had remained completely intact. Let's not kid ourselves. It's a very formidable wall that separates us from our shadow, and I am still working on further tearing down that wall and getting to the other side.

Hemingway may be a tragic example of what can happen if one maintains a formidable persona throughout both halves of life. The persona is to the psyche what the wall was to Berlin. They are both thick barriers that separate us from ourselves and keep us from becoming what we are meant to be. Some walls are more impenetrable than others. Hemingway's was never really penetrable. I think he became a victim of his own myth about himself, his carefully crafted persona that portrayed him as a hero who was tough, courageous, unyielding, stoic, adventurous, hard-drinking, and hard-living, a womanizing lady killer who was bigger than life. He was always portrayed as *über* virile with a love for hunting, big game fishing, and other activities thought of as signs of masculinity. He told big tales and tall lies to foster this image. When he returned home to Oak Park after World War I, he gave talks that inflated his war experiences. He wore his uniform around town, long after things were returning to post-war normality. But most of all, he wanted desperately to be designated and acclaimed as the greatest writer, indisputably number one. He struggled and fought, as if by doing so he could control the subjective literary opinions of critics and others who read him.

I also suspect that Hemingway wanted the public to identify him with the heroes of his books, characters like Nick Adams in *A Farewell to Arms*, and never with those characters who were weak, cowardly, self-deprecating, overly sensitive, or introspective. Of course, he contained all these qualities to some degree, but he hid behind the *über* virile persona to the end.

Hemingway wrote most of his great books in the third person. That, of course, created distance between him and his characters' various weaknesses and failings. I wonder whether, if he had written more of his work in the first person, we might have gotten a better idea of who he actually was? That may be wishful thinking. Knowing who we are and revealing it are two different things. Disclosure is extremely difficult under any circumstances.

Hemingway fought all his life to maintain the myth he had so carefully crafted about himself. Even after winning the Nobel Prize, he couldn't bear the least criticism that might raise a question as to who was the greatest writer. Younger writers were pressing the boundaries, and critics began to deprecate his work and praise the work of others. Even Edmund Wilson, a famous critic and writer and one of Hemingway's early advocates, became very critical of Hemingway's later work. When Hemingway was asked to review James Jones' book, *From Here to Eternity*, he fell into a rage and savaged the book. He couldn't bear anyone else's writing being deemed even close to his in quality. He simply had to be "the one" and would say or do increasingly outrageous things to make himself appear in the guise of the myth he wanted to project. The wall of persona remained intact, without his ever deconstructing it, until the final shot undid both self and his persona. Even then the shotgun blast was in keeping with his virile image.

In *The Old Man and the Sea*, the old fisherman, Santiago, had landed a huge fish, an achievement in Hemingway's milieu equivalent to landing the Nobel Prize. And no sooner had he caught the fish than the sharks, metaphorically the critics, eviscerated his achievement with their repeated, cold-blooded attacks. Like Hemingway at the end of a life of hard work capped by a grand achievement, the old man lay spent and exhausted. Like the old man, Hemingway could ask what, after all that, he had to show for his labors? Gone was the admiration and respect he had longed for. When nothing important was left, what was the point in sticking around, unless you enjoyed humiliation? Death could be seen as a relief from it all. There might well have been more angst, depression, and pain involved in hanging around than in leaving.

I suspect that his failure to tear down the wall of persona, or at least to make enough cracks in the wall to reveal what lay behind it, especially his feeling side, contributed to his suicide. The maintenance of the wall became a costly, painful, and dangerous burden to him. Still, it is possible that he would rather have died than to have given up the powerful persona he had spent his life constructing. Perhaps suicide was the only route home that he could imagine, the only means he could see to relieve his aching yearning to be there.

While I was a practicing psychoanalyst, I dealt daily with patients with suicidal ideation and impulses. It can be scary work. One never knows when someone under one's care will slip quietly down to the basement, as Hemingway did, and kill himself. While I have many theories as to why people commit suicide, including those I applied to Hemingway, I am certain I don't really know why. I doubt the person committing suicide really knows why. It is likely one of those mysteries that only God knows. None of that, of course, keeps us from imagining the reason why. I also suspect that Hemingway's death at his own hand seems more tragic than most of the thousands of suicides that occur each year. How could someone who had recently won the Nobel Prize, who had achieved so much in his life, take that life, and plummet, like Icarus, from the heights to the depths in a matter of seconds? On the other hand, who are we to say that any one life is more valuable than another, no matter how high that person had climbed or how low they had sunk?

It's actually quite humbling to realize and acknowledge that we really don't know the "why" of much that happens in life. We have all kinds of theories as to why someone dies of a heart attack or cancer or AIDS. We assign reasons for someone's illness, their smoking, diet, or lack of exercise, whether they engaged in some sinful activity. Then, we reflect on someone like Churchill, who lived to an old age with many of those bad habits. It's very hard to admit that we really don't know.

I suspect that my deep curiosity about Hemingway and his life may be a kind of warning signal to me. While my actual achievements in the world are minuscule compared with his, I still suffer a harsh drive for achievement, much like that of Hemingway and his character Santiago. If there is an unconscious wish for achievement that is more important than one's life, the only hope for safety would seem to be inner work that might reveal that truth to us.

Let me come back briefly to the question raised earlier as to whether any one life is more valuable than another. The question arises often when a famous and important person dies and their loss is widely mourned. A recently released movie called *Worth* actually deals with this issue. The movie is about the attempt to determine the relative worth of the lives of people lost in the collapse of the twin towers for the purpose of reimbursing families for their losses. For example, do we pay the family of a firefighter lost in the conflagration more or less than the family of a wealthy stockbroker? This issue of the relative importance of people makes me think back to one of the most critical tasks we had in my business and, in fact, in most businesses. We constantly faced the challenge of keeping our business staffed with workers who had the right mix of skills and knowledge needed to operate the business successfully. We needed plumbers, electricians, engineers, bookkeepers, salesmen, and janitors. I was responsible as the head of the business for making certain that our staffing was adequate for the job. At some point, however, the thought intruded that the business would fail very quickly in the absence of people with so-called "mundane" skills. On the other hand, If I were absent for months, the business would continue to run. It wasn't that I was unimportant, especially in the long run, but that my importance was quite relative and not as crucial as I had once thought. We needed almost everyone, high and low, for the business to operate well. I also learned that if we got rid of all the liars and petty thieves and everyone with a drinking or drug problem, we would fall well short of our need for competent people. We might have had to get help of one kind or another for these people, but the truth was, we needed them.

Then, I thought that if the staffing problem for a business was a challenge, I couldn't imagine the scope of the task of staffing the world with the mix of people necessary for it to function, at least, to function tolerably well. Such a task is monumental, and there is no central planner for that as there is for a business. It's too complicated. We've seen the limits of central planning for a nation in many Communist experiments. But somehow, the world ends up with enough plumbers, electricians, carpenters, tailors, cooks, garbagemen, accountants, secretaries, clerks, engineers, sign painters, tellers, glass blowers, and so on for it to muddle by. There is also a reasonably sufficient range of IQs. My take is that all the complicated work and thought necessary to staff the world is done by the Creator, or whoever or whatever we want to call the entity smart enough to create the world and sustain it.

We have to know our shadow in order to know who we are. We also have to know our shadow if we are to escape a fate like Hemingway's. The shadow, as mentioned earlier, is a Jungian term for that part of us that contains all those qualities we don't want others to see or even suspect are there. We attempt to hide this part from others, and often from ourselves. The shadow's qualities are mainly found unacceptable to parents and to our collective, conventional society. My cursory reading of *Faust* many years ago left me with the impression that Faust's pact with the Devil involved a kind of permission to enter, live, and experience the "shadow." I also have the impression that Faust's deliberate experience of the shadow reflects Goethe's belief that Christian orthodoxy and bourgeois pedantry keep us from an area of life that is actually needed if we are to achieve our full potential and if we are to feel truly loved.

How can we believe it when someone says, "I love you," if we have hidden large areas of ourselves from them? To believe that we are loved under such circumstances is, I think, delusional. If we want to be loved unconditionally, we have to reveal ourselves unconditionally. The question is, "Can we ever succeed in doing that?" All we can do is try, accepting that we probably won't get all the way to our goal. At least we have the satisfaction of feeling more loved than we were when we presented a very limited revelation of ourselves. Unfortunately, in this game of strip poker, our anxiety will mount with the removal of each piece of clothing, no matter how tiny, because we simply don't know at what point the loving will cease. Some of those who were told that they were beloved when they were fully clothed will find, after revealing their secrets, that they are still much loved, while others will not be so fortunate. Much depends upon the capacity for tolerance of the beloved.

Actually, I'm reminded here of a joke I once heard. A man was on a talk show and was asked how long it had been since he had had sex. He replied, "Twenty years." Incredulous, the host asked how that could be. The man replied that twenty years ago he and his wife were going to have sex, and, when they got undressed and saw each other totally naked, they began to laugh so hard that they couldn't do it.

The need to know and experience shadow contents in order to know ourselves and achieve our full potential confronts us with a painful dilemma. Maybe I should say that life confronts us with this painful dilemma. We find ourselves caught between our human aspirations to grow, develop, and achieve and our equally human need for love, which we put at risk if we do what is necessary to effect that growth and development. If we have to enter the shadow in order to grow, we are dangerously entering a realm that, from a Christian standpoint and probably also from mother's standpoint, is the realm of the Devil. This is not conventionally acceptable. For these reasons, among others, the shadow is a forbidding boundary to human experience and perception. It is true that we cross the boundary at our peril; it is equally true that we fail to cross it at our peril. It's the way Berliners felt about the wall. Maybe this is another reason that "*Ich bin ein Berliner.*" I feel the same desire to cross my wall — and the same fear of crossing it — that Berliners felt regarding theirs.

Caught as we are between a profound need to be and to express ourselves and a deep need to be accepted and loved by others, we struggle daily between the fear of losing ourselves and the fear of losing others. We search for creative ways to thread the needle of that dilemma. We may remember and sense that the struggle between ourselves and others may be related to our primary experience of mother. Only a single letter of the alphabet, "M," separates "mother" from "other." The profound need for mother's love and our failure to get enough of it fuels a lifelong search for love that affects, often from a deep psychic background, all we say and think and feel and do. The difficulty in separating from the mother that I portray here is in itself a paean of praise for her and her enduring place and importance in our lives. She is a lifelong counterweight that helps us develop ourselves. Because we need and want her love, she is also one of the great catalysts the Self uses to further creation. Viewed in this essential role, there is little basis for complaint, no matter how good or bad she may have seemed. And it broadens our perspective if we remember that Winnicott (1971) defined the good mother as the one who is just good enough.

The imagined agony and ecstasy of being and expressing one's self is what makes me say both, "thank God for the persona" and to curse it, all in the same breath. I often blame mother and others for keeping me from being myself. Sometimes, I think I could be myself if I just weren't surrounded out here in Oklahoma by all these fundamentalist, self-righteous, narrow-minded, unsophisticated, prejudiced, anti-intellectual, extraverted, conformist, sociable people. Then, I think what a lie that is. My inability to be and express myself has nothing to do with where I live or the mix of qualities of the surrounding people. I could live in Berkeley or Boston or Cambridge or Paris and I'd have the same struggles. I would still be adaptive, just in different ways. I would just hide different things. Besides, I'm just as narrow-minded, self-righteous, and conformist as those I criticize. No, there are other reasons why I can't be myself and fully express myself. I live behind my own Maginot line because I am afraid. As long as I need to be loved by others, I will fear venturing out from behind that line. I'll just hide different things from different ones whose love I want. And there is one other reason. Our self is simply too complicated and too unconscious, too beautiful and too ugly, too evil and too good, too smart and too dumb, and too filled with paradoxical opposites and ironies to ever be fully known or expressed, even if the wish to do so existed, which it doesn't. At least, the wish to do so and be so runs head on into the opposing wish to not do so or be so. Our own contradictions stand in our way. But it is all this that also makes us the incredibly beautiful works of art that we are. Despite all of the art and literature that attempts to represent us, it still isn't us. It's a metaphor for us. And these attempted representations of us are never as beautiful or artistically and creatively complete as we ourselves are, just as representations of Berlin can never capture the depth and complexity of its mystery.

It is our shadow and the wall we build to hide it that keeps us from fully knowing and expressing ourselves. Expressing all of it can feel like an unbearable risk to the love we need from others. In order to know and express ourselves completely, we may have to become willing to be crucified and condemned by those we love. Or we may escape the tension the way Hemingway did. Most of us never resolve the tension either way. We simply live with it, hiding just enough of ourselves to remain acceptable to those whose love we need.

Sometimes, however, we stumble into our shadow serendipitously and accidentally, when we aren't even consciously looking for it. It's as if we've found ourselves on the other side of the wall without knowing how we got there. On a trip to Paris, my wife and I saw a painting we both loved. On the wall of this museum was a fairly uncomplicated modern painting that consisted mainly of a few bright colors plus the boldly emblazoned words: *mon envie: d'être le seul.* My wish: to be the one. Nancy's first reaction when she saw the painting was to exclaim, "My God, that's what your book is about." She was referring to a book I had just finished before coming to Paris. The title of my book is *Eighteen East 74th Street,* and an important theme in the book is my own wish to be *le seule*, to return to being "the one," the only one my mother worshipped until I was dethroned by my younger brother. I had lost my divine right, and I mourned the death of the king, that is to say, my own death.

Soon after seeing the painting, Nancy and I began somewhat humorously but also lovingly to say occasionally to each other: *tu es la seule* or *le seule*, as the case may be. "You are the one." Long after we had returned to the States and had continued repeating this phrase to each other, a very powerful thing happened. I said to Nancy, "*Tu es la seule,*" and this strange look came upon her face. With a gleam she said, "Do you mean *tu es la seule* or *tuez la seule*?" That is, "Do you mean 'you are the one' or 'kill the one'?" Almost the moment she said it, I could feel that there was something very profound about her insight. I wasn't sure exactly what that profundity was, but I sensed in my bones a deep truth.

The first connection that entered my mind was Herman Hesse's (1927/2002) book, *Steppenwolf*. It was a book in which a man was following a kind of Jungian process of individuation. To reach his goal, he had to kill the anima, the one most dear to him. In Hesse's book, the hero has been developing a relationship with Hermine, a beautiful, sensuous, and seductive woman. At some point, the hero says, "How gently and inconspicuously she cast the net I longed for around me, and how playfully... she gave the sweet poison to drink" (p. 167). "I belonged to her wholly" (p. 203). Jung described how this happens to us as we do the inner work and encounter our feelings, the anima within. She can get us in a lot of trouble and lead us to do things we would have thought crazy. At midlife we may be tempted to have extramarital affairs, change jobs, drop out, or become the artist or writer or chef we'd secretly longed to become. Jung mentioned that his encounter with the anima had led him to think of going to Paris and getting a garret apartment where he would write and paint.

After a long and playful time with Hermine, the hero recalls Hermine's earlier statement that she had "one aim only in making me her lover, and it was that she should die by my hand" (p. 203). The hero carries out her wish and kills her by stabbing her in the breast.

When I first heard my wife's insight about killing *la seule*, my memory of *Steppenwolf* was still vague. I had read it forty years ago. So, for weeks after hearing her insight I would ask myself, "What on earth could it mean to kill *la seule*?" Then I had an insight about a possible meaning. I had the thought that this is what God ordered Abraham to do, to kill Isaac, his most beloved son. God did something similar. He sacrificed or, at least allowed to be sacrificed, his only begotten son.

Hesse's killing of the anima reveals a painful truth we may have to face in life. Until we find the true God, our Self, in Jungian terms, we have to keep killing our false gods, everything we have made a god, everything we have made most important, whether it be mother, father, family, sweetheart, career, wealth, power, or status. We even have to let go of our wish to be *le seule*, to be loved the most by someone else. Anything except our Self that we make most important serves to separate us from our Self. Life is a continuous process of having to let go of something previously important to us so that we can move on to the next essential stage in our development. Even the trapeze artist, dangerously high above the circus floor with no safety net to catch him or her, must let go of the first trapeze in order to grab the next one and complete the performance. In the case of Hermine, from the hero's perspective, the anima had done her work. She has connected him to his shadow, the place in him that, like all of us, holds his darkness, but, like dark earth, is rich with possibilities. When this happens, she has finished her work, and he has to let go in order to grow by digging in the dark earth. It's in the shadow that we find our Self, and her sacrifice has led us there.

I think the term "killing," as used in this case, is meant symbolically and psychologically. God insists on being *le seule* or *la seule* or both, that is, God insists on being the only surviving love. He's what we end up with when all other loves have failed us. The New Testament suggests this idea when Jesus says: "If any man come to me, and hate not his father, and mother, and wife, and children, and brethren, and sisters, yea, and his own life also, he cannot be my disciple" (*King James Bible*, 2021, Luke 14:26). He also seemed to want to be *le seule*.

We can imagine that the path to God goes through graveyards strewn with the corpses of false gods. My book, *Eighteen East 74th Street*, is also about letting go of things that are most important: mother's love, money, prestige, fame, and so on. Even at the end of that book, I am still struggling to let go of my desire to acquire a mansion, which had become extremely important to me.

I also became aware that my wife's insight included a truth that collectively is very old. The Celtic rituals of killing the King are founded in this truth. It's related to the Buddhist idea of shedding all desires. It is the path to Nirvana. I'm reminded of the thesis I wrote while in training to become a Jungian analyst in Zürich. I called my thesis, *Letting Go: A Prerequisite to Personal Growth and New Life*. Even then I was aware that finding God or, in Jungian terms, finding our Self, involved letting go of many things that had previously been of greatest value and importance, that had provided security, status, and even meaning. Eventually, it means letting go of life itself, which, of course, is the thing that really remains *le seule* or *la seule* until the last. That is the final letting go.

This line of thinking also helped me realize long after the fact why, for an alcoholic, letting go of alcohol is a spiritual experience. Alcohol has become the most important thing in an alcoholic's life. Unconsciously, it has become God. That's why they say in Alcoholics Anonymous to "let go and let God." I also realized at some point that, while some of the deep shame I felt about my alcoholism was related to its violation of conventional norms and its characterization as sinful in my mother's eyes, the deeper reason for the shame was that the unconscious knew that I had made a false god of alcohol and that it had become the most important thing in my life.

That's why we attempt to hide our most shameful behaviors and keep them secret to the best of our ability. There is a connection between secrets and sacredness. Our secrets are sacred because they eventually connect us to God. The most sacred things are kept out of sight, at least until some critical point in life when we deeply and urgently need to see them. The Ark of the Covenant was hidden behind many veils. Eventually, according to some legends, it was said to be buried deep in the Sahara Desert at Tanis, though there are various scriptures and legends about its location and eventual reappearance. Only the elect in many religions are allowed to see the most sacred. Shame is paradoxically sacred, because to face our shame and the thing we are most ashamed of can only happen with the help of a spiritual experience. The shameful thing has become so powerful that it literally dominates the way we think and act. It has become our higher power, and we need the help of the truly Higher Power to let go of the shameful thing that has us in its iron grasp. After I got sober in Alcoholics Anonymous and began to live a more meaningful and satisfying life, I can remember thinking that I actually felt grateful for having become an alcoholic even with all the suffering it had involved. Without the suffering and the shame, I likely would not have had the spiritual experience that was essential to release me from alcoholism. Still, I have to remind myself here that not everyone who recovers from alcohol has a spiritual experience. Some who recover say they were never aware of a spiritual experience. Of course, my feeling was that they had one but just didn't know it or couldn't name it. But who is to say? Perhaps we should take them at their word.

Whether they had a spiritual experience or not, all alcoholics I have known experienced much shame as a result of their drinking. They also tried desperately to hide their alcoholism. It turns out that the shameful thing that we hide is both sacred and profane. All truths possess this kind of paradoxical and contradictory aspect. Mircea Eliade's book, *The Sacred and the Profane* (1987), is a beautiful and profound exposition of the close connection between these two opposites that has existed since the beginning of time.

It makes me think back on the strong propensity for secrecy that existed in my family, which I inherited. My family attempted to shroud itself in secrecy. I suspect that's what happens to all families that have an alcoholic parent. In my case, it was my father. We were ashamed of him and how he looked and dressed and behaved. We didn't want others to see us as we were. We were ashamed of all that comes in the wake of alcoholism: loss of jobs and income and the ensuing inability to pay bills, to take care of the house and the property, to have enough food and clothing, as well as the tearful pleadings, the incontinence, the smell of dried urine and feces, and the loud and angry arguments, which were often followed by fights that wrecked the house and dishes and furniture. Who wouldn't try to hide all that? As a result, we never had company except for other family members.

Of course, these dark secrets were not all that secret. Perhaps some of the most shameful behaviors were successfully kept secret, but in general, all our neighbors and many in the community knew my father was a drunk. They could see him staggering into the house on his way home from the taverns. And the close neighbors probably heard the loud arguments. They certainly witnessed the growing deterioration of the outside of our property, if not the inside. I'm sure we naïvely thought our secrets were more secret than they were. That satisfied our need for a comforting delusion, because it would have been too humiliating to think otherwise. We did everything in our power to maintain the delusion.

This pattern of trying to keep shameful behavior and conditions secret took residence in me and became a lifelong habit. The last thing on earth I wanted to be, or even appear to be, was anything like my father, and I put enormous thought and energy into hiding any of my behaviors that would make me appear to be like him: lazy, irresponsible, unkempt, unreliable, dishonest, poor, dumb, weak, dependent, selfish, incompetent, undisciplined, or licentious. I never wanted to have a drinking problem and felt sure that was a weakness I would never have. But the hiding may also be a result of something in our unconscious that senses that there is something sacred about the shameful behavior so that, paradoxically, it must be kept hidden, like the Ark of the Covenant, so that we can later have the spiritual experience that comes from finding and seeing it.

Despite all my wishes to the contrary, I eventually developed a serious drinking problem. It became my biggest secret. I couldn't imagine anything more humiliating. For years, I hid it quite successfully. I never missed work and was very good at my job. Fortunately, early in midlife, not long after I began having blackouts, forgetting where I had parked my car, forgetting conversations, and behaving in an embarrassing way at parties, I had a spiritual experience that saved me from the worst thing I thought could happen to me. This experience came quietly. It was the day after one of my worst drunks and hangovers. I apparently had blacked out about four o'clock on a Sunday afternoon. As I was told the next day, I drove a friend to the airport. I had no memory of that. I was also told that later in the evening I went to the back door of a neighbor's house and loudly tried to lure his good-looking wife into the back yard. The only moment of consciousness I had that evening was when her husband came to the door and shouted at me. I ran, tripped over the sharp-edged stone that formed the border of their garden, and came down so hard on my head that it popped the lens out of my glasses. If I'd come down an inch closer to the stone edge, I would have been impaled on the sharp stone and killed. My wife somehow got me home and put me in a tub of cold water. I was so hung over the next morning that I got her to lie for me and say I was sick and wouldn't be at work. As I think about all this, I doubt I have the capacity even to imagine how difficult it was for my first wife to live with me. I was a bad husband and a bad father, especially when I was drinking. I wish I had been better. On the other hand, if I had been better, I would have been someone else. I'm not comfortable with that idea either.

That day was actually, and, as I look back, surprisingly, the first time I missed work because of drinking. Later in the morning I went down to the basement to be alone and think about things. That's when the spiritual experience came to me.

Not a thousandth of a spiritual experience can be described in words. It's too numinous. It's too powerful and it's too brief, and in many ways it is actually unwise to tell others about it, especially if they have never had such an experience themselves. It's not their fault. It's a human limitation that absence of experience insulates us from knowing certain kinds of things. The truth is that you do feel special when you have such an experience. But if you tell others about it, they can hear it as a bragging statement of your specialness. They can also think you are weird, perhaps even delusional. So for years I only spoke of this at Alcoholics Anonymous meetings, where there were many people who had had such experiences of their own.

The experience itself happened like this. I was sitting in my basement, alone, very tired and depressed, feeling a sense of frailty and failure. I was feeling helpless to do anything about what seemed a complete shattering of my life as I knew it. I heard the words "God help me" escape my lips. Almost immediately the experience came.

One reason why a spiritual experience is so hard to describe is that the experience is more of a feeling than a thought. It's a feeling that there has been a sudden and total inner shift and reorganization of values and attitudes. That isn't true, but it feels that way. The shift has altered your sense of yourself in many ways, but by no means totally. You know you are still basically the person you were when you were five years old but that now you have a very different perspective. Part of you seems to be gone and something new has taken its place. The old feeling of self doesn't go away; it's just diminished and has less influence on the direction of your life.

While thinking about this spiritual experience, I find myself remembering other, similar experiences in my life and noting they all came, not when I was enjoying some peak of success, but soon after I had failed at something important or had been sick and was feeling weak and helpless, the way we must feel when we are babies. It was in those vulnerable moments that I called out for God's help and it came. It's as if God responds to a helpless adult the way a mother responds to a helpless infant. There's something about the weakness and frailty and helplessness that triggers feelings of sympathy and an impulse to help, both in mother and God. We feel saved. I felt saved not after a big success but after a huge failure. It's ironic, as I had come to believe that God and mother reward successful behavior and stellar achievements, not failure. On the other hand, neither mother nor God can or will always respond to plaintive calls for help. If they always responded agreeably, it would for us be the same as being God. But, something more important may have engaged their attention: an injured sibling, a fire, a flooding basement, an earthquake. Still, I would feel hurt at the seeming neglect. After all, who or what could possibly be more important than me and what I needed?

It was very soon after this spiritual experience that the thought of going to Alcoholics Anonymous came to me. I found myself remembering a conversation I'd had with a car salesman whose locker was across from mine at the YMCA. One day a couple of years earlier he had said to me something that at the time seemed completely out of the blue, that if I ever had a drinking problem, I would do well to go to Alcoholics Anonymous. He explained that he had had a drinking problem and found Alcoholics Anonymous very helpful. I wondered why he would say that to me. It seemed totally irrelevant. Given the experience of my father, I thought I would be the last person on earth ever to have a drinking problem. Fortunately, however, the conversation somehow took root in my subconscious and came to me during an hour of need. I decided to give Alcoholics Anonymous a call. They told me the days, times, and locations of meetings and offered to send me some literature. I didn't take them up on that, as I didn't even want the mailman to see it coming to my house. Talk about false pride! That's a pretty good example. At the meetings, I did find plenty of literature, and I took it home, where I kept it well hidden. Incidentally, the salesman who gave me the saving idea about Alcoholics Anonymous showed up at my house just after I had begun to go to Alcoholics Anonymous meetings. He arrived under the guise of wanting to help and especially to be helpful to my wife. The "help" he offered was to try to seduce her. My wife told me about his attempt. I suppose he is also an example of the sacred and the profane being two sides of the same coin.

One of the hardest things I ever did in my life was to stand up in Alcoholics Anonymous and say, "My name is Larry, and I am an alcoholic." What would have been impossible for me in any other setting was difficult, but still possible, in Alcoholics Anonymous. After all, I was saying it to others who I had heard admit this truth about themselves. They weren't altar boys, and they admitted even more dark truths about themselves quite openly. I got to where I could do that, too.

Alcoholics Anonymous helped me in a number of ways. I felt an unburdening from the unpacking of many of the secrets I'd spent my life hiding. In Alcoholics Anonymous, it's much easier to confess your alcoholism and all the dark behaviors that go with it. You can confess without being judged, since the others who are hearing you are in the same boat and have done many of the same things.

In fact, I learned from my experiences in Alcoholics Anonymous that keeping dark secrets is a two-edged sword. They have to be kept long enough to create the tension that produces the spiritual experience that releases you from them, but not so long that they become a threat to sobriety and, perhaps, sanity. In AA, you are encouraged to share those secrets with others. Confession also serves our profound need for intimacy, the need to reveal ourselves completely to and feel completely accepted by another human being. Of course, no one can be completely accepted by another human being. No human is that saintly. But you can feel a level of acceptance never before experienced in life. Confession received without judgment feels like an experience of unconditional love, even if it isn't entirely so. We simply cannot feel loved for who we are without revealing the "good" and the "bad," since both good and bad is who we are. If our self-revealing confession is received without judgment, we may also experience forgiveness.

While the keeping of secrets can be important and helpful in some ways, it can also poison us. Sins and secrets have a close connection. Getting them into the light can be curative. Confession, done when the time is right and the ego can somehow bear ugly truths, is a healing principle in most twelve-step programs and has long been an important part of effective psychological work. It was borrowed from religion with good reason. In psychotherapeutic language, confession is called "catharsis." In some ways, it does the mind good, much as a cathartic does the body good. It cleans it out and helps us discharge and dispose of psychic toxic waste. Confession is one of the most important parts of our toxic waste disposal system. Writing this book is part of the same disposal system.

Alcoholics Anonymous members are encouraged to make moral inventories of their "sins" in writing and to admit to themselves, to God, as they understand him, and to another human being the exact nature of their wrongs. The process softens the sense of isolation and helps heal their loneliness and their guilt by connecting them to others who have been suffering secretly in the same way.

To help members in their process of confession, there is another step in the twelve-step program that involves writing down all the people they had harmed and all the shameful behaviors they could remember. When I did this, it was quite an unburdening, and there is no doubt I gained a lot of serenity and inner calm from this step. Of course, I was never completely open with others outside Alcoholics Anonymous, but I became more open as my Alcoholics Anonymous experience made me more comfortable with my wayward thoughts, feelings, and behaviors. At some point, I became quite aware that I still had a deep secret that I couldn't share even with Alcoholics Anonymous members, who themselves often confessed to unbelievably selfish, sordid, and wicked behaviors, including some that were illegal. Later, I will talk about that secret.

It was from reading Jung that I learned that there is a connection between alcohol and spirituality. As a result of his long experience as a psychiatrist, he had come to believe that alcoholism was a mental disease that could not be healed by psychotherapy. At some point he realized that those who did get well did so as a result of some kind of spiritual experience. He sensed that alcoholics when they drink are not really looking for alcohol; they are looking for God. The drinking is simply a misguided effort to find the spirit in the bottle. That's probably why we call alcoholic drinks "spirits." Jung's formula for the treatment of alcoholism was *spiritus contra spiritum* (Jung, 1961, p. 3), literally "spirit against spirit." He believed that a spiritual experience was the only cure for alcoholism. Eventually, when an alcoholic would come into his practice, he would tell him at the beginning that he could not help him and that the only solution he knew of was a spiritual one, and that the quest for that solution might be aided by going to an Oxford Group, which was in many ways the precursor to Alcoholics Anonymous. Jung (1961) himself had some influence on the development of AA, as his exchange of letters with Bill W, the founder of AA, suggests. Jung also knew that while there were things you could do to be open to a spiritual experience, there was no way to make a spiritual experience happen. When it came, it was a gift from the grace of God.

Despite what Jung wrote, and in order to present as objective and balanced a view as I can, I should add that in my long experience in AA and as a psychoanalyst, I am aware that AA isn't for everyone. It has helped millions, including me, to become sober. Still, some alcoholics resist it. They may find the idea of a higher power too religious and unacceptable. They may be uncomfortable with group dynamics and the inevitable politics that are present. Alcoholics take many paths to get sober. Some go to church, some turn to psychotherapy, and some do it on their own. Both church and psychotherapy can provide a setting where confession without judgment can be received and guilt ameliorated. Drugs, in some cases, may provide a helpful bridge into sober thinking. However, most alcoholics probably never recover in any setting. I continue to feel that some kind of spiritual experience occurs in sobriety no matter what path is followed.

At a deep, inner level, the sacred and the profane are united by an underlying reality that acknowledges their interdependence: the truth that neither one has any meaning without its seeming opposite. Without the contrast provided by the profane, we could not become conscious of the sacred. We hide our sins for the same reason that we hide and keep out of sight what is most valuable, like the Ark of the Covenant, so that thieves will not break in and steal our treasure. When we become conscious of how sacred our "sins" are, we can bring them into the light and share their sacredness and their worth. Jung himself believed that the shadow, where we hide our "sins" in secret, is ninety percent pure gold.

The "sins" we commit, along with the guilt we experience from them, eventually catapult us onto a path that leads us to psychological as well as spiritual development. The path leads us to our Self, a Jungian term for the totality of our being and a psychological construct for God within. It also leads us to pain and suffering that we seek to assuage.

Churches that denounce sin might notice, if they read sacred texts honestly, that what they are denouncing is the very thing that would bring people close to God. The New Testament is quite clear that Christ hung out with sinners rather than with the righteous.

So our shadow contains both our sins and our gold. We can't find one without the other. If we want to find what is in our shadow, we have to develop a relationship with the unconscious. I've spent most of the second half of my life trying to do that, but it's difficult to want a relationship with something that is not only rich and beautiful but can also be terrifying and ugly. We can also view it as a huge, deep ocean that we must navigate, first in its shallow waters, then moving deeper and deeper.

I had a dream that helped me see something important that is needed, if we are to navigate it safely and well.

> I am at a marina in Zürich. I have gotten on a boat that looks like a Downeast design. It isn't my boat, and I am about to go out in it without the permission from the owner. I start the engine and begin to move forward. I know how to handle it because it is like the boat I had on the Chesapeake, but I am worried about damaging someone else's boat. I scrape something on the way out of the slip. Then I immediately notice that the direction I want to go is actually a series of rapids that look very rocky and dangerous. I turn back and look for another way through. I see further back to my

left a possible opening that might lead around the rapids, but I conclude it won't get me there, either. This isn't like anything I'd ever seen in Switzerland.

First, I take the water in the dream as a symbol for the unconscious, and I am trying to navigate through it. The biggest problem, I think, is that I am in a boat whose owner is Swiss. The Swiss are noted for being stiff, orderly, conventional, and rational. Those aren't qualities well suited to navigating or even attempting to navigate the unconscious. A Swiss boat might get pretty damaged by the rapids. It might even sink. To navigate the unconscious, we need something quite different from the conscious Swiss mind. What we need in many ways is exactly the opposite of the conscious Swiss mind.

There are brief times when the Swiss mind is suited for navigating the unconscious. One is during *Fasnacht* or *Karneval*, when even the Swiss bankers don their masks, dress in outrageous costumes that are anything but buttoned up, then march around half drunk, tooting horns and generally behaving and speaking in ways that are quite unacceptable in polite society. I was told when I was in training in Switzerland that people are so uptight that there has to be this occasional mass chaos in order to avoid mass suicide. Of course, the Swiss are wise to give themselves this outlet, where they can let go and let off steam before they explode. They also have rituals for their children to let off steam, something the children need as much as their parents do, because Swiss children also lead an extremely orderly life. For example, in a U.S. doctor's office, we often see children loudly running about, yelling and playing. In Switzerland, you rarely see this. They sit upright with good posture and in total silence when in a doctor's office with their parents, usually their mother. If a Swiss child does get noisy, often an older man will go over to the mother and say something like, "*Bitte, bringen sie ihre kinder in ordnung.*" "Get your child under control." Their children have to be very well-behaved and orderly or they are severely punished. In many Swiss households, however, each month they have a ritual in which they give the children rubber baseball bats, and they are for a brief period allowed to hit each other and their parents with the rubber bats.

Our relationship with the unconscious begins and develops very slowly. We have to learn to accept our irrational side because to enter and relate to the unconscious requires a change in attitude like the one the Swiss undergo in order to enter Fasnacht. Their mind has to open to a different way of thinking and acting and experiencing life.

Perhaps the first thing we have to do in order to become open to the unconscious and to make ourselves willing to go there is to become conscious that the unconscious actually exists. Something has to make us realize that we are not the only one in our psychic house, that there is another part of the house that we have at best even vaguely known was there. Initially, this can be a shock, because often we have never been consciously aware of any of its other inhabitants or consciously experienced anything about this part of our psychic house even though we may have expressed it or even acted it out at times. In my case, I thought my conscious self was the entirety of my own psychic house, until I had a terrible failure and a spiritual experience that saved me from it. It was my first experience of the "other." It was an irrational, inexplicable experience that eventually opened me to this whole unexplored part of myself.

In order to explore the unconscious, we have to do some things that may seem weird to others. We may enter therapy. We may experience dreams, which can help us in this exploration. They can even give us information that can provide guidance for our outer lives. It's like the nautical discovery of the sextant and longitudinal and latitudinal charts. Both oceans require some special tools to navigate. Dreams become like our sextant, our guide to navigating the unconscious. But really rational people, people who have never had these psychological experiences, look at us the way they look at hippies, especially if we say things like, "my dreams were telling me to......" Before I had my own inner experiences, I thought of people who said they had spiritual experiences in this same way, as if they were talking so much gibberish and booey hooey. Fortunately for me, my experiences now keep me from making this kind of criticism.

Accessing the unconscious also requires getting in touch with the feminine, feeling side of ourselves. We need the feminine to relate to the other. It is more tolerant and inclusive. It helps us relate to others and frees us from our haughty isolation. The feminine also helps us relate to our intuition, which is important but usually less valued in our rational paternalist society. We tend to value thinking and sensation more. We have to suspend the conventional Swiss part of ourselves and embrace the Fasnacht Swiss side of ourselves if we are to enter the unconscious shadow where the feminine, in many of us, especially men, has taken refuge.

Those of us more thinking oriented had access to our feelings, to our feminine side, at the beginning of life. Thus, it's really not a discovery of feelings I am talking about. It's a rediscovery. There was a time in our life when we were much closer to our feelings and better related to them. In childhood, we could experience a much fuller range of feelings, both the positive and the negative. We could know we were angry or disappointed or unhappy and express it. We could say to our parents that we hated them. We could also be openly loving and affectionate, unless it was rejected. We could say we were happy or that we were sad. One of our most intense early experiences of feelings was with mother, when she looked at us adoringly with unconditional love, as if she were seeing the first sunrise. Very soon, however, socialization began, and a wall went up that separated us from our feelings. Our feelings went behind that wall, and after that we lost contact with the feeling side of ourselves. In our effort to succeed in a paternalistic world that values thinking and reason over feeling, we tried to become boys and then men, immersing ourselves in the realm where thinking dominates. We were even taught that feelings are dangerous.

Wagner's Ring Cycle is a beautiful portrayal of the struggle between thinking and feeling. The ring gives power over feelings by giving the masculine thinking side power over the feminine feeling side. It accomplishes this by giving the masculine thinking side dominion over women's capacity to create. If we are cut off from feelings, we are cut off from the very thing that leads us to our creativity.

The domination of feeling by thinking leads to a tragic loss, which, if we are lucky, we can correct later in life. Our obsessions can play a critical role in the rediscovery of our feelings, if we use our imagination to follow them to the end. If we follow the obsession to its end point, feelings are there, metaphorically the same as our first experience of feelings with mother. Now we experience the feelings as belonging to us, rather than to mother or to some other person or thing we thought was supplying the feeling. We find that what we feel belongs to us and is caused by something inside of us, rather than something outside. We can see this phenomenon in our relationships. We fall in love with a woman. Time passes and we fall out of love. We no longer think she is so beautiful or charming or sexy. But she hasn't changed. So, the feelings we had for her initially were our feelings. She wasn't making us feel the way we did; we were making ourselves feel that way. And we prove that to ourselves when we fall in love with the next woman. We've carried the feeling with us because it was always ours. Women can have the same experience falling in and out of love with men. The identical experience also exists for same sex love.

We become obsessed with what is missing in our lives, not with what we have. Therefore, later in life we become obsessed with things that bring us in contact with or trigger our feelings. The trigger may be love for a woman or a man or for music, art, money, or success — or, unfortunately, for drugs and alcohol. But the purpose of the obsession is to connect us with our self, which contains our lost feeling. We start with an outer image we are obsessed with, be it money, grand houses, music, sex, or success, and let the image progress in our imagination until it takes us to the deepest inner image that is our Self. And when we find ourselves, we find our feelings. This process of following an outer image to its deepest meaning is described by Jung's prescriptions for active imagination. Proust (1925/2003) wrote by a similar process which he describes in detail in volume six of *In Search of Lost Time* (pp. 253-330). I have wondered if he learned it from Jung or if Jung learned it from him. Perhaps each found this method separately.

Descartes' "I think, therefore I am" reflects the pervasive attitude in highly rational western societies. Here, rational thought is sacred. Thoughts trump feelings as the respectable guide for decisions and action. Feelings are treated as inferior and are seen more as nuisances that have to be tolerated than as helpful providers of direction for our lives. Still, the discovery by Descartes that there was a thinker inside his head that defined who he was, or who he thought he was, is very important. I've read that every truth contains something in it from the very beginning. I suspect thinking is a good example of that. It must have been there from primordial times, and every thought we have today is connected to the original thought that occurred thousands of years ago in our evolutionary past. Rodin's sculpture, *The Thinker*, probably touches us so deeply and gets its power from the evolutionary depths it represents. The main problem I have with Descartes' statement is that it doesn't go far enough. There is more to who we are than thinking. There is feeling, which was also found in our primordial beginnings and, like thinking, is connected to every feeling we have today.

In sharp contrast to their subordinate role in the patriarchy, feelings play a very important role in the Jungian model of psychological growth. Jung came to regard feelings as the stars that light the path to the Self. This was particularly true of feelings that use our likes, dislikes, and interests to guide us and keep us on that path. Access to these feelings becomes, in Jung's view, essential for psychological development and for making good decisions. Guilt associated with the expression of feelings, particularly those unacceptable to the ego and conventional values, is a formidable obstacle to our full development, because painful guilt causes us to bury many feelings in the shadow, temporarily moving those painful feelings far enough away from consciousness to give us some relief, at least for a while. The high valuation that the Jungian model accords to feelings is not generally shared in our society.

In Jung's work on psychological types, he concluded that thinking and feeling are psychological opposites. When one is dominant, the other is repressed or split off. This is more often a problem in us men. The struggle between thinking and feeling produces enormous tension. The integration of opposites, including these two critical ones, is essential to psychological growth. At the same time, Jung was quick to point out that the trick is to gain access to our feelings without throwing our thinking out. Thinking is also enormously important, but in a different way.

Feelings are accessed by a woman in the feminine core of her being and by a man in his anima. Both men and women may have resistance to feelings. In a man, the resistance to this feminine quality comes from his masculine ego. In a woman, the resistance to these feminine functions flows from her animus, the masculine part of herself, which is in conflict with her feminine being. Deep within the man's psyche, there is a "she" who does this work, if he can find a way to be open to her. A woman is more naturally open to feelings and relatedness, even if her ego is dominated by the masculine animus, because her being is at its root feminine.

Many of the barriers to accessing and expressing our feelings are quite commonplace and encountered in our daily lives. To be judged successful by many in the outer world, we at a minimum need to leave home, get an education, marry, have children, pursue a line of work, be respected by our peers and colleagues, pay our bills, and provide financial security to our families. This is a collective standard that puts much pressure on us. The wish to achieve all these goals, or more, inhibits our behavior and especially the expression of our feelings in many ways. For good reason, we are afraid to express openly our negative feelings about our boss, company, or organization. We need a job and maybe even a promotion to reach important goals. Similarly, we may be reluctant to express feelings openly and honestly in our relationships for fear of losing them. Having good, or apparently good, relationships is important to feeling successful in life. The struggle with the expression of feelings persists through most of our lives. And we look for ways to relieve the pressure.

It is difficult for the ego to accept that there is something outside of and unknown to itself that can provide the creative direction needed to find and assemble properly the stones needed to build and complete one's creations, one's life, and one's self. This is one reason it is hard for the conscious ego to trust feelings. For the ego, it is like turning the direction of one's life over to something that is alien. To trust these feelings takes far more faith than the ego usually can muster. This may also be why the feelings must work by seduction and/or gradual desensitization to draw the ego to what it needs. This may be why Jung said that we can either go along voluntarily or be dragged. The Self does not care whether the ego goes along or not; but if the ego does not go along, then the feelings, the Self's agency in building the personality, must become wilier and wilier and, sometimes, increasingly forceful, to get the Self's work done. While it may sound implausible to think that feelings and interests can guide us in this way, it's worth noting that our egos accept quite easily that some animals, such as whales, turtles, and penguins, have an inner sonar so precise that it can lead them thousands of miles back to their breeding grounds.

Feelings are essential to creation. Our feelings and emotions supply the temperature changes that can connect and fuse two psychological opposites, two antagonistic psychological molecules, to form a new psychological compound, just as temperature changes can help form new chemical compounds from separate and antagonistic molecules. The new compound contains both of the previously separate molecules and yet is neither of them.

The new compound is synergistic, something greater than the sum of its parts. It can be a strong marriage or a fragile marriage, just as we see in outer relationships. If the ever-shifting emotions and the associated changes in temperature go away, the compound or the relationship may break apart again into its separate components. The idea of synergy from the marriage of opposites is captured in the following poem, which I wrote several years ago for two friends in Zürich who were getting married:

Synergy

Synergy's a wondrous thing.
It's magical and mighty;
Bound together by a ring
And blessed by Aphrodite.
Un et une sont plus que deux.[2]
Fusion brings a great release,
Latent heat and energy,
Out of war has come the peace.
That is also synergy.
Un et une sont plus que deux.
All is built from single cells
That lived in isolation.
Come together like two bells
To ring in celebration.
Un et une sont plus que deux.
City, state, nation, world
Yield one's precious sovereignty,

---

[2] One masculine plus one feminine equals more than two.

Now a broader flag's unfurled,
Ever greater unity.
Un et une sont plus que deux.
John and Catherine, un et une,
Toute ensemble, plus que deux.[3]
Fusion sun et lune,
Beau mariage de tous.[4]
Un et une sont plus que deux.

We see the same process at work in nation building. The original thirteen colonies which formed the United States often had separate and antagonistic interests. One has only to read about America's founding to sense the enormous feelings and emotions that supplied the changing temperature necessary to form this new, synergistic political compound. The feeling and the emotion that provided the feeling levels necessary to bind these antagonistic and separate entities are evident in the speeches of Patrick Henry (Wirt, 1817) and Thomas Paine (1776).

Feeling and emotion can also break things apart. That is part of creation, too. Emotional temperature, cold and heat, resulted in the American Civil War. It created the fission that split the old Union and the fusion that created a new one, both enormously powerful events. Feeling also was essential in the breaking apart of the former Soviet Union into independent states. The point is that change in temperature can bring about

---

[3] Together more than two.
[4] Lovely marriage of all.

changes in substance, and the temperature changes required to bring about psychological change are supplied by feeling.

While in Alcoholics Anonymous I became able to reveal, as I did as a child, much more of myself, my feelings as well as some sordid secrets. There was one secret, however, that I could not utter out loud in AA or even when I was alone. It was something that happened when I was very young that brought me joy at a time when joyful feeling was completely absent in my life. But the joy led to a behavior so shameful that I had kept it secret all my life. My suffering was comforted somewhat when I realized that what is most secret is also most sacred.

I committed incest when I was twelve years old. From the perspective of a ninety-year-old, I am quite aware that all incest is not the same. I think now that the incest I committed was a rather innocent initiation into the sublimity of sexuality that was precipitated by surging hormones that yearned poignantly for expression. We were about the same age. We loved each other, and I don't think a power dynamic was involved. In some respects, these early adolescent explorations of sexuality felt numinous, and one of its main attractions was that it was about the only great pleasure we experienced at a very bleak time of our lives. We'd just come out of the Great Depression, we were in a world war, we were still very poor, and times were tough. We were hungry and afraid, worried about having enough food and clothing. In my household, there was little love, certainly no hugs, terms of endearment or other outward expressions of affection. There was no joking or light banter. There were no children's books or reading of stories or fairy tales to the children. No games were played. Cards were viewed by my grandmother as sinful. Her cold and puritanical attitudes dominated my home. So, the pleasure of this experience was in such contrast to my drab, cold and rigid existence that it overwhelmed the usual inhibitions that would normally oppose such behavior.

I also know from my experience as a psychoanalyst that incest can seem quite evil when it involves a power dynamic, generally speaking, when an older family member exploits a preteen or young teen.

Despite the enormous pleasure and even the sense of numinosity that flowed briefly out of the experience, it had a deep, long term psychological effect on me that was felt primarily as profound shame and guilt. Unexpectedly, something from time to time would trigger memories that undermined my feelings of self-worth, tormented me, and led to secret suffering for most of my life. I knew or felt somehow that it was wrong even though I don't recall hearing the word incest or specific admonitions against it ever spoken in my home. Feeling it was wrong was not enough to keep me from doing it. The exhilaration of temptation in the moment was the complete opposite of the remorse I felt afterward. Apparently, the biology of desire was so powerful it completely suppressed any sense of morality, but once desire was spent, the suppressed guilt returned with a vengeance.

I couldn't imagine it could be any more pleasurable with someone I wasn't related to, even if it were considered less wrong. At the time, knowing it was wrong, deeply so, didn't affect how it felt at the moment. It was a very intense feeling that wasn't supplied by anything else in my milieu. You'd think something that bad for you just couldn't feel that delicious. If you eat some spoiled food that is bad for you, you know it's bad almost the second it hits your mouth. There's nothing good about it. Eating spoiled food isn't a sin. But what I was doing at twelve years old was. And it wasn't very long before the guilt began to drown out the good feelings, until it eventually ruined them. Eventually, I realized that incest isn't just any old sin. It's so bad that society places an enormous taboo on it.

The guilt I felt was likely not only about incest but also about sex of any kind. In my house, especially for my puritanical grandmother and to some extent for my mother, sex was simply a sin. My grandmother referred to women who got pregnant out of wedlock as "hussies," but she also applied the same word to women who wore dresses or shorts that were too short or who wore too much lipstick. It didn't take much that was suggestive or sensuous for them to see it as sinful.

It took many years of therapy and analysis to sort out my own emotional flip-flops. For a while, I thought the good feelings before sex were authentically my own and that the feelings afterward were based on what I was taught, what others felt and had imposed on me. The good feeling, I thought, was the way sexuality was in the beginning, before Christianity, before religion of any kind had put the brakes on many kinds of behavior, even seemingly harmless behavior. Now, however, I suspect that both the feelings before and after were my own.

The opposites exist in our Self to create both consciousness and meaning. What we feel has its roots in the contrasts between opposites. For example, if I live in Miami and drive from one side of the city to the opposite side on a warm winter day, I'm not aware of the heat. I'm not conscious of the pleasantness of the warmth. But if I fly in from Toronto in the winter, the heat feels wonderful. Contrast is essential to feeling. If a roller coaster ran on flat ground only, we'd get little sensation from it. But when it drops precipitously from a slow ride up, we feel the thrill. If we get in a hot bath, after a few minutes we are not conscious of the warmth, but if we lift our bodies up into the cool air, the water feels hot again. The contrast provided by opposites is critical to human consciousness. I suspect this is why I felt both so good and so bad about my childhood incest experiences. The existence of one feeling depends upon the existence of the other. To have the rainbow, we have to have the rain. The more conscious we become of life's ambivalence and the more tolerant we become of its ambiguity, the better adapted we become to life and the better we live it. The pleasure of the incest seems somehow to be related to these contrasting opposites.

When I got older, I realized this sex had been so much more powerful than the recreational sex that I later experienced many times with other women, and I wondered why. I think the difference in the strength and depth of feeling is explained, at least in part, by several factors. One difference is the feeling of love that was present in my incestuous experience that was missing in recreational sex. It is also missing, as I have indicated, in incest when the power dynamic is present. That kind of incest doesn't bring anything even remotely like pleasure to its victims. In the incest I experienced, I loved her. I thought she was very pretty, and she had a terrific personality. She could play the piano by ear like a virtuoso. I came to realize how much more powerful sex is when it is with someone you love. Recreational sex is pleasurable, too, but milder by comparison. Recreational sex is more like a beer high; sex with someone you love is better than hard liquor.

Later I heard all the talk about royal families and incest and how that closeness in blood relations, even first cousins, leads to mental defectiveness and even physical flaws.

I heard those tales even before I went to Zürich to train to become a psychoanalyst. While in Zürich, I read a book that claims a more important reason for the incest taboo (Layard, 1977). The author believed it is society's way of assuring that blood is invigorated and renewed by requiring marrying outside the tribe. It not only brought in new blood but also new ways of thinking and acting. It's so much easier to just stay home and have sex with relatives. The taboo forces us to be willing to do the work needed to search for and discover partners outside. This diversification of blood enriches the culture in many ways. I'm glad I didn't know all that when I was twelve. I suspect it would have diluted the experience.

The incestuous experiences were pretty short lived. They just seemed to fade away. I suspect my partner in crime had found boyfriends to absorb her interests and energy. I had also reached the age when I got interested in girls and got together with them at parties and eventually dates. I had also matured enough sexually to make the experience risky from a practical standpoint. Very early in life I became conscious that an unwanted pregnancy would torpedo my growing ambitions to succeed.

When I'm not feeling guilty about the incest, though, I can actually sense something spiritual about it. The idea that sex, and especially illicit sex, can feel spiritual is not what they taught in Sunday school in those days. It was more often quite the opposite. Sex, and especially sex outside of marriage, got associated with the Devil. And incest is even worse than simple fornication. Others have recognized the spiritual, even sacred, nature of incest. The propinquity of the sacred to the profane is not a new idea. It is not only contained in our sacred texts but also in great literature. Thomas Mann's book, *The Holy Sinner*, portrays the sacredness of incest that is forbidden by our most powerful taboos.

I suspect that the reason incest can touch spiritual depths is that it brings us so close to our self. We define incest as an intimate relationship with someone closely related. The closer the relative, the more powerful the taboo. We think of sisters and brothers, mothers and fathers, even cousins as representing the ultimate taboo. But who could be a closer relative than our self? That's what we do when we penetrate the shadow; we have psychological intercourse with our self.

Recently I had a dream whose imagery provides a powerful example of sexual penetration of the shadow that is psychologically very accurate. In some ways the dream is so beautiful that I am willing to risk the personal embarrassment involved in revealing it. Here is the dream:

I am alone in a strange room. A young man
unknown to me slips uninvited into the room.
He feels threatening and dangerous. I grab
hold of a metal file used to sharpen blades. I
turn it so that the sharp piece where a handle
goes is pointing toward the intruder and try
to jab him with it. I'm feeling impotent as I
can't reach him with the jabs. My arms flail.
Then, he takes out what I think is a knife. I'm
very afraid. I grab him and try to take the knife
away. While wrestling we come close together
and our groins meet. I feel a sensual rush that
appears to be leading to a sexual encounter.

The young man, of course, represents my shadow.
Initially I feel what most of us feel when we encounter the
shadow side of ourselves. It is scary. We resist it initially but
find ourselves helpless to resist its lure. Our Hermine often is
the seductive lure who both leads us to and connects us with
the shadow. She is not afraid of the dark stuff. She knows we
need it if we are to live fully. We find there forbidden fruit
that not only can give us pleasure but also enrich and deepen
our lives in other ways. Though we try as hard as we can to
live upright lives, we succumb to this dark side of ourselves.
We find a layer of ourselves that we couldn't acknowledge
consciously was there. It's what happened to Faust at midlife.
It's what happens to many of us at midlife. We find, as the
Germans found, that underneath the orderly, logical, rational
facades is a layer that at its depth contains not only Dionysian
chaotic pleasures but also feelings, intuition, and boundary-

breaking creativity. Of course, it's not just the Germans. But they fit the picture beautifully.

Of course, the dream is also a picture of symbolic incest that seems necessary if we are to connect to parts of ourselves that we need for our own growth and development. What could be more incestuous than sexual feelings of one part of our selves with another part of our selves, as the dream portrays? Or more sacred or spiritual? I have come to think that incest has connected me not only with my spirituality but also, through contact with my feminine self, with my creativity. The Self for me is another word for God the Creator, the entity representing the totality of creation.

When we produce a "child" by means of our creative work and our art, the archetypal model of creation may be closer to the phenomenon of the virgin birth, in which conception and birth occur spiritually without the benefit of physical intercourse. The process by which creative people get "pregnant" with their works similarly depends upon an unseen spirit, which many artists throughout history have called "holy." For creative people in general, getting pregnant involves a kind of psychological incest or androgyny which can only be experienced in an inner psychological and spiritual way. In fact, Jung believed that it is this "incest" that dreams and fantasies were pointing to, rather than incest in actuality. This symbolic incest, he believed, is the prerequisite to psychic rebirth and creativity (Jung, 1956/1976, para. 565). I believe this phenomenon helps explain the creativity I experienced writing several books.

Symbolic incest occurs in all creative work. All creation requires some kind of intercourse between the masculine and feminine opposites. This is an outer reflection of what Jung called the *hieros gamos*, the sacred marriage. In the *hieros gamos*, there is no physical phallus or vagina. It is a spiritual marriage of the inner king and queen, representing the marriage of the archetypal masculine and feminine. It is the psychological consummation inherent in creative work that brings us in proximity to, and causes us to embrace, the opposites. This psychologically incestuous intercourse brings opposites together and produces intense feeling. And it produces a spiritual pregnancy in which the child that is born is an artistic creation. Any artist knows that feeling that arises at the "aha" moment — the production of something new. Wherever the opposites touch, they not only bring consciousness of feeling, but also activate the Creator, as if the Creator dwelled in that tiny gap, in the borderland between them. Often at their beginning new creations or new ideas are deemed to be taboo. Impressionist art is an example. I wonder if part of the reason for that is that the tabooed creation is itself produced by a process that is incestuous in nature and taboo. The incest that is taboo in the outer world is essential in the inner world, if we are to create. Of course, there is a huge difference between inner psychic incest and actual incest.

Because incest of the inner type connects us, at least symbolically, to our Self, it is also important to our process of individuation. The ultimate goal of individuation is connection to the Self. All through life we have episodic experiences of our Self. Those are moments of high feeling that are similar not only to the "aha" moment of creating something but also to actual sex, as well as other things like profound insights, unusual achievements, and even drugs and alcohol.

Being true to ourselves may bring about a backlash from society. There is probably nothing more threatening to the dominant forces of the collective society than someone truly being himself or herself. That may be an unstated taboo that is even more powerful than the incest taboo itself. Being fully one's self is not acceptable in almost any society because it expresses so much that lies outside the cultural and societal "barbed wire fence" that is erected to keep out unconventional ideas and developments. Joan of Arc, Gandhi, Christ, Socrates, Copernicus, Galileo, Darwin, and other audacious people were truly themselves and pushed themselves far outside the fences that had been built around their particular societies, cultures, and religions. But their ideas were frequently deemed unacceptable, if not dangerous, and they were often attacked and, in some cases, killed. The findings of scholars and scientists who introduced and developed scientifically acceptable evidence that eventually supported Darwin's new idea of evolution are still under challenge today, just as they were when the theories of evolution were first introduced. The theory of evolution that is accepted by the traditional scientific community today was originally not accepted by the established science or religion of the time. Thus, evolution started outside the fence and eventually moved inside the fence.

Although incest isn't explicitly forbidden by the Ten Commandments, I think it wreaked its own kind of vengeance on me. For most of my life, I suffered painful neurotic guilt from the experience. It contributed to the feeling that something was wrong with me. I think it was part of what made me feel like an outsider all my life. People don't usually share their incest experiences with others, so it's easy to feel you are an odd one who has done something bad that others don't do. Those feelings were ameliorated somewhat when I became a psychoanalyst and learned otherwise.

I later drew some comfort from understanding the inner incest's role in creativity and individuation. On the other hand, the individuation process itself contributes to the feeling of being an outsider, someone different from others.

Learning that you are not the only one who has committed a particular "sin" also provides some comfort. I remember a good example of how that comfort worked. When I was in junior high, my good friend Bobby would occasionally invite me to spend the night at his house. Each time I would wake up with this wonderful, orgasmic sexual feeling. I never initiated it, but I also never objected as it felt too good. But I felt guilty afterwards, as I did after all sex, and worried about being homosexual. One day I was talking with my best friend Gene, also a friend of Bobby's, and something caused him to say, "Yeah, it's like spending the night at Bobby's." I didn't say a word back, but I can tell you I felt an indescribable relief knowing that I wasn't the only one experiencing this with Bobby. Both Gene and Bobby have been dead for years, but I'll likely never forget either the experience with Bobby, or the kindness of Gene's words, despite Gene's never knowing I had experienced his kindness that way.

While my violation of the Ten Commandments didn't make me feel as bad as incest did, I violated so many of them that I suspect the cumulative effect also added to my neurotic guilt. The neurosis comes from feeling you are alone in your badness, that you are a moral freak. Because I violated so many of the commandments, the history of my trespasses spans many years, not to mention the present. In truth, I violated every commandment, except murder.

Adultery for me began pretty early, when I was around fifteen. It continued to occur intermittently until later in life when I fell truly and deeply in love. It was only then that I realized that if you really love someone, you don't want to have sex with anyone else. It's not a question of having to exert will power or clinch a bone between your teeth in order to resist the temptation. I realized I simply didn't want to. I also believe that what happened to me is another example of my particularity being a universality. I believe most people who truly fall in love are not with their partners for many of the usual reasons like status, economics, religious beliefs, or even shared interests. They are with them because of feelings. They may have shared interests, but that isn't the reason they are together.

So, let me remember that what I so strenuously tried to keep secret was not my successes in life or my stellar qualities like hard work, intelligence, and reliability, but rather my failures, the many times I exhibited immoral and "sinful" behaviors or succumbed to qualities that my mother frowned on like laziness, unreliability, dishonesty, drinking, and sex. I felt she was only proud of me and that she would only reward

73

me with love and admiration if I made good grades, went to college, and became a big success, especially by making lots of money.

The truth is, however, that the few times in life I experienced the most profound feeling of being loved by mother (whom I once felt was God) was when I behaved in those just-catalogued disreputable ways that I tried to hide. Briefly, while I was still an infant, mother adored me. I felt loved unconditionally despite the fact that as an infant I was a mess. I was the opposite of what I later thought yields love and admiration. And in those few spiritual experiences in which I felt saved by God, it was also when I had exhibited immoral or negative behaviors that I had come to believe God punished rather than rewarded.

All this brings us back to the fundamental question as to whether we are loved, even saved, by either our high achievements or our abject failures and human weaknesses. Later in life, I came to feel that my mother didn't love my father because of his alcoholism and all the unseemly and disapproved-of qualities that went with it. But I was forgetting the pain I felt as I lay in the cradle at the foot of their bed and heard my mother and father making love, moaning and whispering sweet endearments. The pain came from my feeling displaced by my father. Previously, in earlier infancy her look of adoration had made me feel like *le seule*, the only one, but now this love-making scene annulled that. Many have read in psychology texts the clinical, sanitized versions of this terrible experience. But those texts are as far from the real thing as being in a deadly auto crash is from reading about one. I was so upset that they put me in my grandmother's bed, where I stayed until I was ten years old, and I was so traumatized that I didn't speak until I was five years old.

The primal scene is primordial, occurring at the beginning when all was unified, when the opposites had not yet been split in two, when they were side by side, instead of one after another. At that point the two sides of creation existed together, just as they did in a unified Berlin, construction and destruction side by side.

The infant observing the primal scene does not have the equipment necessary to process and understand these opposites side by side. He cannot see the ravaging of mother and the creation of new life as one thing. The totality is too much for him to bear, so the more painful, destructive side is split off. The infant is split by the trauma of the incomprehensible, and the virgin and the whore, the constructive and destructive opposites, are split off.

But the experience of the *ur-Szene* can also lead us back to ourselves. It's a long journey back to that incomprehensible and unbearable instant, the *ur-Szene*, in which the Self in all its power revealed itself in the *hieros gamos*, when the king and the queen fucked, creating a moment of cosmic orgasm, shocking and yet so beautiful that we spend our lives obsessively groping our way back to it. We make progress with the aid of magical mirrors and baby-step desensitization that in the end makes the side-by-side uniting of opposites bearable, enables us to bear to look upon construction and destruction side by side. Berlin also contains all this beauty and destructiveness side by side, if we look carefully and deeply enough. If we envision Berlin as it is, we envision our Self.

The psychic trauma of seeing opposites side by side before your mind is sufficiently developed can be seen in the German movie, *Never Look Away*. A beautiful but very sensitive young girl has been chosen to hand Hitler a bouquet of flowers when he visits her village. Soon after giving him the flowers, she develops a psychosis. I suspect that happened as a result of seeing Hitler up close and noticing that Germany's supposed savior is also evil. It would be like seeing that Jesus was also the Devil. It was shock to her young mind and led to a traumatic mental break. I think the damage is similar to what occurs when the primal scene is witnessed.

My not talking until I was five years old was probably the result not only of the trauma inflicted on me by the primal scene but also of a kind of revenge. I caused my mother and father and other family members much pain. They worried that their hope for a golden boy might be shattered by my turning out to be a cretin. I remember to this day when I first spoke. I walked from our house to my uncle Cloyce's, three blocks away. I knocked on his door, and, when he opened it, I simply said "hello" in a deep voice, turned around, and walked home. The news was so exciting that the wires burned up, first with a call from my uncle to my mother reporting the miracle, followed by calls from my mother to all my other aunts and uncles. By the time I got back to the house, I was greeted with big smiles of relief. I don't know why I decided to spare them the anguish I had been putting them through, letting them off the hook, as it were, but I can tell you that, warm as their response to my "recovery" of speech was, it didn't compensate for the loss of love I'd felt that drove me to silence in the first place. I felt I never again received from mother that brief look of adoration that I will never forget. But by then I was assuming, perhaps incorrectly, that I could win her love in another way, by abandoning the behaviors I had expressed as an infant and adopting a whole set of new ones, a show of high achievement.

Although that early look of adoration from mother was exquisitely poignant, I came to think that "that look" was a much lesser expression of love than her giving her body so wholly to my father. Action spoke louder than looks or words and aroused deeper jealousy in me than her giving "that look" to someone else. Daddy was doing the only thing I could imagine as the ultimate expression of love from momma. One can imagine Oedipus knew this quite well, at least unconsciously. I also wanted to do what father was doing but was completely helpless to make it happen. Sex with others, sweet and lovely as it may seem, could never equal imagined sex with mother. The true *hieros gamos*, the sacred marriage, is between the king and the queen. The king is only the king when the *hieros gamos*, the sacred coupling, is between mother and father. I would have to be the father to be *le seule*. Some kind of unconscious knowingness led both Oedipus and me to this view. I wonder if he saw from his cradle what I saw from mine? But it is mother, not me, who decides who *le seule* will be. I doubt one can feel more helpless than when the choice is completely in another's hands.

If Yahweh was there at the beginning, then jealousy was there as well. Yahweh is the model for jealousy, and, if we believe we were created in Yahweh's image, even in a symbolic or metaphorical way, we got our jealousy from him. It makes me wonder if Yahweh saw his dad doing it to his momma. It must have taken something very traumatic, like my experience of the primal scene, to precipitate Yahweh's terrible jealousy. And Yahweh's jealousy is not a mild form of jealousy. It is not only incredibly and pathetically childish, but also potentially abusive and dangerous. Remember what Yahweh is reported to have said in Exodus 20:1–5: "And God spake all these words, saying, 'I am the Lord thy God… Thou shalt have no other gods before me…. for I the Lord thy God am a jealous God, visiting the iniquity of the fathers upon the children unto the third and fourth generation of them that hate me'" (*King James Bible*, 2021). Jealousy seems to be such an important quality that God not only gave it to himself, but has also passed it along to all he created. Its importance to him becomes even more apparent if we imagine that the quality is as painful to him as it is to us and that he has to bear the pain as we do.

In such matters, we can only speculate as to why he would think jealousy is of such importance to his creation that he embedded it in everyone, including himself. One could easily imagine that if anyone were to be free of jealousy, it would be God. What is there for God to be jealous of? He is presumably omnipotent and omniscient, even perfect. So, it is a great paradox that he would also have many of the human emotions like jealousy, insecurity, and anger. Still, there must be something that makes him feel insecure. Otherwise, why would he broadcast the existence of his jealousy so widely and use it to threaten us with such severe punishment if we fail to regard him as the one and only God? His jealousy seems centered on some rival who might be a threat to his being "the one." He wouldn't have needed to give this dire warning unless he believed there actually might be someone or something else with qualities sufficiently desirable to threaten his position as number one. In the period of Exodus, that might have been ancient deities like Marduk, Ra, or Aaron's Golden Calf. But this suggests that even Yahweh had inner doubts and was so insecure about his own lovability that he had to issue threats to assure he would be loved. It's very hard to comprehend all these contradictions.

The word "jealousy" suggests a wish to have something we don't have but that someone else may possess. If God is jealous, he wants something that he doubts he possesses. It's hard to believe that God isn't certain he is God. But if he is jealous, logic suggests it is so. It's really quite amazing. He apparently planted in us the same uncertainty that he has. Why would he do that?

For one thing, it keeps us from thinking we are God. I suspect very strongly that there is in our unconscious a wish that is the opposite of our feelings of helplessness, of our human physical and mental limitations, of our disappointments in our inability to fulfill ourselves, of our vulnerability. Such a compensating opposite would seem to me to be expressed in the unconscious idea of ourselves being God. And that compensatory wish remains in the unconscious because we would think it is crazy if we consciously thought so. But in our unconscious is the wish to wear the crown, the royal diadem, to be looked upon as Jesus was by the Magi and Mother Mary. Our conscious expression of our wish to be number one in our outer life is a reflection of this unconscious wish to be the God of our world. Let's face it, jealousy is an unadulterated reflection of our profound wish and need to be "the one."

Actually, we have the unconscious wish to be "the one" again. We were "the one" for a very short period when mother first looked at us and adored us as if we were the one, the only one, with an unconditional love that lasted only briefly — in fact, only until socialization began. This feeling of wanting again what we once had is expressed quite beautifully by the painting "*mon envie: d'être le seul*," "My wish: to be the only one," that I discussed previously.

Wishing to be the only one means that we keep trying to recover the feeling that goes with that look of adoration from mother and will try to achieve everything we think is necessary to get it again. It leads to a life of striving. And maybe that is why God embedded into us the wish to be the one as well as the jealousy that is unleashed when anything suggests we are not the one—not so that we would become God, but so that we will strive to become God. It keeps achievement and creation going. And that may be expressed in myriad ways, in writing and composing and sculpting and dancing, but also in more mundane ways like cooking and sewing, knitting and building cars and houses and buildings and recovering minerals from the earth. Plumbers, electricians, and even garbagemen can create and achieve, more or less. Achievement and creation come from a feeling of inadequacy that leads us to keep trying harder. And the feeling of inadequacy in turn arises from the jealous observation that someone else has something I desire but don't have. Jealousy, thus, may be part of the dynamic that tries futilely to free us from the "imposter syndrome" that causes us to feel inadequate despite unrelenting effort that resulted in some evident successes.

In the painting just mentioned, the French word "envie," which means "wish" in French, is the base for our word "envy." So my wish to be "the one" is quite close to a jealous longing. When our wishes are unfulfilled, the resulting emptiness engenders a feeling of jealousy of anyone who appears to have what we lack. In a way, jealousy is the feeling aroused at the moment when we become conscious that someone else has something we deeply want. Jealousy, thus, may be one of our primary inner motivators that leads to creative endeavor, i.e., what we feel we need to do in order to remain the one and to feel loved.

My history of jealousy started early. As I said, I believe it began in early childhood when I witnessed my parents' lovemaking that led me to become mute for several years. My second memory of jealousy occurred in junior high school. It was over my first girlfriend, Carol. I was fourteen and really loved her. One day a couple of years later I was coming out of the high school door and noticed her standing on the corner about a half a block ahead, smiling and talking animatedly with Harry who was a friend of mine, a great athlete, tall, well-built, and fairly handsome. I felt an immediate wave of jealousy and suspicion come over me. My reaction was to never speak to Carol again. I feel sure the objective truth is that she still loved me and that her talking with Harry was just a friendly conversation. She was friendly with everyone. But at the time it felt to me that she liked him and that they might be arranging a tryst. Hearing myself say it now, I know how crazy it sounds. Carol, I feel sure, could never even guess why I quit speaking with her. But not speaking to someone who offended me was an early response to trauma that I had learned would punish the offenders.

In any event, a few months later, Harry came to me and said, "I notice you aren't going with Carol any more. I would like to ask her out if you aren't interested in her anymore."

I just coolly said, "Sure, it's okay." I was concealing my deep hurt and lying to Harry. But I simply could not speak the truth to either of them. The sane part of me knew how crazy my interpretation of their conversation was and would sound. I mooned over Carol for months but never tried to have a real conversation with her about it to simply ask for clarification. That was a far more reasonable way to respond, but I couldn't get the strength or courage to do so.

The next serious jealousy I remember is with Jean, a classmate who really liked me and made it clear that she did. Thinking how much she liked me gave me a feeling of security. And she was very popular, smart, and wealthy. Mother definitely approved of and encouraged this relationship. My connection with Jean gave me a feeling of status among friends and classmates. My feelings of affection for her were not strong, but I think the safety of her liking me, and my feeling confident of her feelings, gave me some emotional security. But the truth was I liked a girl named Ginny more. I just didn't act on it because of an uneasiness about ruining my relationship with Jean. So I would see Ginny with other guys and feel jealous even though I didn't have the courage to let her know I liked her or to act on it.

Jean and I dated off and on for many years. When she found out I was going to Harvard, she applied and got accepted to a nearby college. We were both good students and studious. I was working twenty hours a week in a school cafeteria, so we didn't have much time to get together, but we did see each other every month or so. In the summers, I usually remained in New England to work and save money for the coming year. Jean would go back to Oklahoma. One summer between junior and senior year she took a road trip out west with her nanny and a chauffeur. She invited a friend named Jim along. I think she had just gotten very lonely in my long absences. All through our long relationship we had both dated others from time to time. She told me about Jim in senior year and said that she and he had become very close. I didn't know if that meant she had sex with him. Jean and I never had actual sex, but we did some of the preliminaries. I had the feeling Jean would be angry if I pushed for actual sex, and fear of a pregnancy also inhibited me. In any event, I felt very jealous when she told me, although I hardly reacted at all to her. I just simply stopped seeing her and began to date a girl from Wellesley. After Christmas senior year, Jean called me and said a friend of hers had seen me at a dance with my arm around someone. I didn't deny it, but I also didn't talk about it. Dating the Wellesley girl was my way of expressing my anger about Jim. As in the case with Carol, I couldn't talk about my jealousy and hurt feelings and try to sort things out in a reasonable way. I concealed my jealousy and kept my hurt to myself, I think because I was ashamed of my jealousy. I felt it was pathetic and felt showing it was a weakness that would make me look even worse in the eyes of others, not to mention a bit crazy.

My relationship with this Wellesley girl also shines another light on the primal scene. Part of the trauma of the primal scene stems from my need to be the one, the only one. The primal scene may also be behind the "virgin and whore split" that I felt and many other men feel. On graduation night, I had sex with the Wellesley girl. Three days later I left for a three-month trip to Europe, a trip paid for by my aunt. The Wellesley girl was very attentive and wrote me warm letters quite frequently. My responses to her were cool. I think our sexual encounter made me feel I was not the first one, that she had had some experience. Of course, it was an unreasonable assumption, despite no evidence of a broken hymen. There are many possible explanations for not having a hymen, one of which she later supplied. When I got back to the states, she invited me to their summer home in the finger lakes. While there she told me a story about being caught in the lines of a boat that was leaving the dock and being pulled crotch first into a pole on the dock. I think she was telling me that to assure me that her not seeming like a virgin was due to this accident. Even though I never said a word to her about my feelings that she had had previous sexual experiences, I feel pretty certain she somehow guessed my concerns and came up with her story about the accident. The story may very well have been true, but I didn't believe it. I felt without any evidence she was trying to "work" me.

This brings me to the virgin and the whore. In high school and college I tended to "love" the nice girls and not even try to have sex with them. I treated them with respect. I had sex with the wilder girls but never imagined marrying them. When I finally did marry at age twenty-six, it would have been virtually impossible to find a girlfriend who was a virgin. I never consciously thought I wanted a virgin, but I am sure that wish was an unconscious undertow caused by my wish to be *le seule*. So, of course, I didn't marry a virgin. I fell in love and we frequently had sex before marriage, but soon after marriage, sex became very tepid, always the same with little passion, and the orgasms ceased. I believe that what happened psychologically was she became mother, I became father, and I found the naughty girls outside of marriage. Somehow, the incest taboo in the unconscious inhibited us both and made our sex life very bland and infrequent. After all, I'm not supposed to have sex with mother, and she isn't supposed to have sex with father. I remember couples who would call each other "mommy" and "daddy." We became mother and father and were blocked. I think many men who stray in their marriage encounter some version of my experience. The primal scene is a picture of the virgin and the whore being the same. It's an image too painful for an immature mind to bear. So, the image is split so that the virgin and whore are sequential rather than side by side. This split is very damaging to future relationships.

The need to be "the one" and the jealousy that reflects that can be seen in an especially pathetic light when I recount that I got to know the sexual history of several women in the course of my life. In fact, I often pressed them for such honesty. I became aware that a few of them had given oral sex to previous boyfriends. I then pressed for oral sex as I felt their having it with previous boyfriends and not with me meant they loved the previous boyfriends more, that I was not "the one." It's similar to the way I felt about mother having sex with father. There are, of course, many plausible explanations for why someone does something with one person and not with another. Several of them resisted my importunities for oral sex. I can remember thinking later it was to their credit that they resisted. Maybe they were sensitive to their own feelings, which had changed over time. And they had the strength to say "no" and protect their integrity by being true to their feelings.

Another example of my jealousy, equally as incomprehensible and pathetic as the other instances I cite, was with my former wife, who died a few years ago. Because of my daughters, I don't want to go into detail except to say I had episodes of jealousy and passive-aggressive reactions to it similar to the way I behaved with Carol and Jean. Only once was I able to summon the strength to tell my wife I was jealous and that this was the reason for my cold treatment of her. Sometimes, the jealousy I felt was so deep, the obsessions so relentless, and the hurt so painful that the only way I could quit thinking and obsessing about it was to work. It partly explains my being a workaholic during all the years we were together.

I was also very jealous with Nancy, my wife today. Early in our relationship, when I felt jealous, I would not speak of it but, as was my wont, would subject her to random and intermittent warmth and coldness that would rival Skinner's treatment of his rats. Nancy endured it painfully and stoically. During the long course of our relationship, however, my jealousy nearly healed. At least it healed to a point where it was very mild and not painful or threatening in any way. The healing was very evolutionary. It took many years of my practicing the desensitization that I taught my patients to use in certain kinds of situations. I started with the revelations and expression of my jealousy in a humorous or a glancing way and slowly built up to the point where I could fully express it in its craziest forms. And believe me, there were crazy emotions. Early in our relationship, for example, I might wake up at 1 a.m. and feel jealous. I would have the idea that she was at an old boyfriend's house. I would actually get out of bed and drive thirty minutes to her condo in Virginia and drive around the parking lot until I either found her car or didn't. Rarely was her car gone, or when it was it was probably because she was spending the night at a girlfriend's or with family. But that's not the alternative that came to mind at the time. I never told her about these nocturnal visits. I knew they were crazy and feared she would break up with me. Of course, I couldn't admit such nutty thoughts and behavior. But the steadfastness of her feelings for me had a depth and sincerity I had never before experienced with any other partner. That led me eventually to trust that she would not abandon me. My growing feeling of trust in her feelings slowly gave me the courage to begin to reveal my jealous feelings and behavior, even some of the most childish and paranoid. She handled them like a good therapist, which she is, mirroring my lunacy and reflecting it back without judgment. It was hard for both of us to handle, but our dealing with it evolved to the point that we could joke about it. So, in my old age the jealousy is finally at a very tolerable level, still there, but mild and no longer threatening to my relationship. It's hard to believe my jealousy endured this long. I suppose that says something about how deep my early wound was, how insecure I was and how deeply I feared abandonment, and how important it must be for nature to have embedded the quality in humans.

As I've tried to review my episodes of jealousy, I am aware that my memory always goes back to romantic relationships. As ambitious as I was, one might think I would have experienced a lot of jealousy at my work, envy of others getting things I wanted. I think my jealousy was not memorable in those situations because I did so well and rose so fast in my career that others were probably more jealous of me than vice versa. It may also be that being number one in order to assure the love of one I love may be much more important than being number one in order to be admired by others. Others' feelings were less important to me than were the feelings of those I loved, whom I wanted to love me in return.

In my romantic relationships, I was a lot like Yahweh. My jealousy was incredibly and pathetically childish as well as paranoid and psychologically abusive, even though I was not physically so. I simply couldn't stand not being "the one." I had a brief, flickering memory of feeling like "the one" when I received my first look of pure love from mother. It felt as if I was the king with the royal diadem. Then I became dethroned by that traumatic scene in my parent's bedroom. Later I was pushed further from that sense of singular love by the arrival of my brother, who I thought stole that look of pure love from my mother. Then by Harry, when Carol was smiling at him. And then by Jim, when Jean admitted her closeness to him. I don't think any of the women for whom I felt jealous rage ever really knew about my jealousy. Perhaps my former wife did, but barely. They just experienced my random and intermittent warmth and coldness, closeness followed by distancing behavior without really knowing what caused it. In this way, I was probably different from Yahweh. He announced his jealousy and his rage and his intent to punish. In that way, Yahweh was much more open, honest, and mature about his feelings than I was. But I'm afraid that is damning Yahweh with faint praise.

Perhaps the most neurotic aspect of my jealousy was that *mon envie: d'être le seul,* my wish to be "the one," is a wish to have something even Yahweh couldn't achieve. And I couldn't achieve it for the same reason that Yahweh couldn't. Who is number one is decided by others and is subjective. Think of all the talk about who is the number one quarterback. We hear heated arguments about it daily on ESPN. Or who is the best writer or painter? Or the richest, given all the hidden assets? There seems to be no way to anoint universally a number one in any area of life, including who is God — is it Yahweh or Jesus, Mohammed, Vishnu, and on and on? The answer is too dependent upon subjectively diverse opinions often shaped by the accident of one's birth into a particular culture, nation, religion, or family. It makes no difference how hard the athlete — or writer or painter — may try to be number one or how good he actually is, whether he is deemed to be number one is determined subjectively by others.

Actually, the wish to be "the one" is the perfect formula for leading both Yahweh, myself, and others to helplessness. Our wish to be the one is undermined by the way number one is determined. Basically, I turned the determination of my worth over to others. And here, perhaps, is the worst part of that. It caused me, and Yahweh, to become separated from our own feelings. Our need to be number one was so great that we became interested only in what others felt about us and, therefore, became unconscious of how we felt about them. We didn't focus on who we loved. We focused on who loved us. And so our feelings languished in soulful neglect.

It was the attention to others' feelings that led me to the incredibly absurd desire to have a virgin, despite the fact that I had had sex with far more partners than any of the women I was attracted to. Just having had sex with one other person caused me to feel my girlfriend had betrayed me, just as my mother betrayed me with only one other man. My need to be "the one" simply made me oblivious to my own feelings and behavior and aware only of the feelings and behavior of others. How could a man like me, who appeared reasonable, be so pathetically and absurdly unreasonable? I'm still not certain of the answer to this question, except to speculate that God made me, and probably everyone to some degree, with a desire to be number one, so that we spend our lives creating and achieving so that others will, hopefully, designate us as "number one." I don't think God wanted us to be the only one and achieve something even Yahweh couldn't achieve. He just wanted us to keep trying to achieve that so we might help him create the unfolding world. Perhaps it was his deep need to be number one combined with the impossibility of his being "number one" that made Yahweh the perpetual creator that he is. He never rests. He suffers from his own divine discontent.

We are given the kind of impossible tasks that the heroes and heroines of fairy tales are given by the witch, and satisfying the witch is always a never-ending task. Is it possible that I am living a fairy tale like the ones we nightly read to our children? Is it possible that we read our children fairy tales so that they will get some understanding of the kind of world they will live in? Are fairy tales a closer picture of reality than we ever imagined?

The more conventional, psychological explanation of the cause of my jealousy is the loss, the grief, and the excruciating pain I felt when I lost my first love, first to daddy and then to my younger brother. After that, I was afraid to fall in love for fear they would leave me for another. The extreme fear led to extreme jealousy which, in turn, led to a need to watch future girlfriends very carefully, like a hawk, for any sign they might have an interest in another guy. It also led me to attempt to control girlfriends and bind them to me by doing for them and giving them everything I thought would make them love me exclusively. Of course, that meant trying to give them everything that I thought pleased my mother — money, impressive houses, nice cars, beautiful clothes, college degrees, titles, elite professions — all the things that bespoke wealth and visible accomplishment.

While I am certain that most people experience jealousy in their lives, I can't explain why we aren't all equally jealous. Perhaps jealousy is distributed in the form of a bell-shape curve as nature distributes many qualities, like height and intelligence. If everyone were at the low end of the curve, the world might be full of sluggards. Or if the weight fell at the other end of the spectrum, it might be full of viciously aggressive and destructive people. Fortunately, nature appears to be more balanced.

I don't think the failure to be *le seule*, "the one," is mine alone. In truth, I think that even God cannot be certain he'll be *le seule*. Others decide that. That's probably why Yahweh had to try to secure his position by threatening to punish anyone who didn't place him above all else. He knew that there were those who thought Ra, Indra, Zeus, Marduk, or stone idols were *le seule*, and this realization made him so insecure in his position that he tried to secure it with threats.

The problem is that God reflects what people believe him to be. They can inherit those beliefs or come to them independently. I suspect the real God, the one left standing when all others have been killed, is so secure in his power and knowledge that he knows he is God whether others believe it or not. He cares about how he feels, not how others feel about him. He doesn't have to please or threaten anyone. He has tenure, can't be fired, and simply doesn't care whether others believe in him or love him or not. Belief changes nothing. And there is nothing you can do to influence God's decisions or get in His good graces. God takes His own counsel and goes about His own business undeterred. Similarly, all those things we do to influence mother, whom we may have believed for a long time was God, are empty gestures.

Let me here offer a brief summary of three important strands of behavior in my life. I have written above about my alcoholism, incest and jealousy. These three qualities and behaviors have caused me and those close to me considerable pain and grief. For each of these qualities and behaviors, however, I have also written about their positive aspects both for me and others who experience these behaviors. I have noted how alcoholism led me to spiritual connections and to a waking up to the other, the previously unconscious part of myself. I suggested that incest, despite the guilt and pain it costs, is necessary, in our inner life, if we are to be creative. And jealousy fuels our drive for creative achievement. All three are also connected to our deep need for love by others, including God. All three are part of our misguided efforts to find the love we seek.

After all our training and all the propaganda we've been exposed to, it's no wonder that we believe that we have to behave in certain ways and achieve certain things in life if we are to be loved. We forget that the only time in our lives that we experienced unconditional love and acceptance is when we were infants and mother looked at us as if we were Jesus. We get that look not only well before we have achieved anything of note, like good grades and promotions or wealth or fame, but also before we had good manners and acceptable behavior. Jesus also got that look from Mary and the Magi before he had worked any miracles or saved anyone.

Achievement and good, responsible behavior are simply overrated as a basis for being loved, so much so that our belief is close to delusional. We somehow are comforted by the delusion that we can do something to cause ourselves to be loved. We see it in a high-performing older child who has lost that look of love from mother to a younger sibling, whom he believes to be a worthless mess. I fear we may have to believe we can regain that love even till the very end. We can't give up trying. Look at me. I'm still trying to write another book. I'm still hoping for some achievement fantastic enough to finally get that love. But I'm trying to get it long after mother has died. So, I must be looking for someone else to love me the way she did. And what could be more naïve than to think another human, not my mother, could give me the unconditional love that mother once briefly did? Grown-ups can only give that look of love to babies. And, as I opined before, it's unlikely that God can be manipulated by some devious means to give us that love.

If the only time we received that love was when we were infants, then maybe the Bible is onto something when it says we must become like a child again if we are to enter the kingdom of heaven. It probably is true that if we became as a child again, and someone said they loved us in that condition of aged senility that is often referred to as second childhood, we might believe them.

But just to show the depth of our belief that good, responsible behavior and achievement are the keys to love, look how afraid we are of becoming a child again. Look at the anxiety we have about our increasingly wrinkled appearance, the loss of hair and teeth, our inability to walk. Look how afraid we are of becoming so dependent that someone has to feed us or take care of us or change our underwear or take us to the bathroom or wash us or put our clothes on for us. Look at the anxiety we have about forgetfulness when we simply can't recall a famous actor or athlete or even the president's name. Then we forget what we went into the other room for, and that sets off more anxious alarms.

To halt this process of decline, we take vitamins and a whole pharmacy of other pills, some of which are supposed to help our memory or halt its decline. Or we do puzzles and tai chi and other activities aimed at helping our memory. We go to the health club. We walk. We do yoga. We eat healthy diets. We cut out red meat. We take mindfulness classes. We join Meals on Wheels and do other things to help others, thinking this may slow our decline. We probably don't admit it, but we are likely terrified at the growing evidence of the setting sun that leads us into second childhood, senility, and eventually death. Maybe I shouldn't say "we." Maybe it is just me. If being allowed to enter heaven is evidence of God's love, then why am I so scared of the very thing that the Bible says is a prerequisite to entry? Why am I fighting with all my might, all the way, to avoid the very condition that supposedly will usher me into love? And then there is the question that, if I hate the idea of becoming a child again and resist its onslaught instead of embracing it, will I be worthy of getting the reward that the Bible says goes with the condition?

Sometimes, I find myself feeling as I did when I learned there was no Santa Claus. I definitely didn't want to give up that belief. Probably none of us did. I felt very lied to and disappointed. But maybe this is an example of why lies can be as important as truth. Maybe that "white" lie about Santa Claus helps us more than it hurts us. One might argue that it is better to have enjoyed that wonderful feeling about Santa for six years than not to have experienced it at all. Perhaps, believing all those lies about achievement and good behavior even until I was ninety was better than not believing them at all. Just having the grounds for hope that I could actually do something myself to bring myself love was comforting and motivating, especially motivating. I worked so hard trying to achieve admirable things that I nearly died at midlife. After that, I worked less hard, but I never gave up the effort to succeed. As I said, look at me. I had a book published when I was eighty-eight, and here I am two years later, working on another. This really doesn't feel like fun. It is hard work. I must still secretly think that if I win a Pulitzer or some such prize, someone will adore me unconditionally for that. Of course, I know better. Listen to me: I sound pathetic. So why doesn't knowing how pathetic all this compulsive effort is slow my efforts or my wishes to be famous, important, and worthy? As you see, I'm working on it. I'm trying to write myself into an answer. Of course, the moment I had that thought, another thought intruded: if I find an answer to that cosmic question, I will be famous for that. So, I march on.

I simply can't stop either the effort to achieve something great or give up the hope of some windfall that would make me seem that way. I can't help it. I still dream of getting amazing things. I had a dream of owning the New York city mansion at Eighteen East 74th Street. I even wrote a book about that dream and the outcome from it. I thought owning such a mansion might cause me to be loved by all my friends and perhaps others. Still, deep down, I know that no friend will ever love me in the way that momma did or give that adoring look I got from momma in that initial, unparalleled glimpse of pure love. The love of all my friends put together can't equal it. But with momma, long dead but the only one whose love counts, why do I keep trying to win that gaze of total adoration?

This question makes me realize that I must be some kind of masochist to continue the quest for achievement and the admiration I came to believe and hope would come with it. It's actually quite absurd to try to achieve status in life in order to get love when it is clear that the only true love I ever experienced as true, pure, unconditional love came before I ever achieved anything. After that brief experience, the unconditional part went out the door, and I had to perform and achieve in order to get even the semblance of whatever love remained. No one should know more about the consequences of the obsessive-compulsive need for achievement than I. As I've mentioned, it made me depressed, sick, and exhausted by midlife. The need for achievement is the source of a midlife crisis for millions of people. That need precipitates the crisis and then comes round again as the not-infrequent hellish fallout that emerges in the wake of the crisis.

My contradictory beliefs about what brings love have shaped my whole life. Mother's first message to me was that you are most lovable when you are a stinking, dirty mess. That was the condition I was in when I got the look that I forever yearned for. I got that look and then lost it to a younger brother. Then, I spent my life foolishly thinking I could recover that look by doing what pleased mother most. The look I got from doing what pleased her never equaled the earlier look, but it was close enough to the earlier look to think that, if I did just a bit more, I would finally get the original look I craved. It became quite clear what pleased her and brought the semblance of the look I sought. She gave me that good, but somewhat diluted, look when I was successful. The profound need for mother's love and our failure to get enough fuels a lifelong search for love that affects all we say and think and feel and do. It's actually very complicated. Mother must have thought that if her son achieved all these admirable things that she too would be loved. So, the message that love depends on achievement spans the generations and probably is passed on as surely as eye color or height.

I actually accomplished much of what I thought would bring my mother's love back to me, what would make me feel once again that I was *le seule*. The truth is that I had deluded myself. All the huge effort to succeed left me stressed, anxious, and exhausted and, even worse, holding an empty bucket. I hadn't won back her love. Of course, the truth is that there is no way to win love. It belongs to the one you want it from, including God, and they can give it where they please. And it is often difficult to understand how others make the choices they do, how they decide to give love here or give it there. It often goes to the black sheep, the prodigal. In my case, it was to my brother. He was a nice person and not a black sheep, but he made poor grades, never won any honors in school, wasn't a good athlete, never made a lot of money, never owned fine homes, or went to a fancy college. He wasn't a fancy dresser. And what's more — and this was infuriating — he didn't even try to make mother like him, let alone love him. When she was down and out at the end of her life, he didn't send her money despite her supplications. Nor would he pay attention to her or sympathize with all her complaints and pleas for attention. I sent money even when I was fifty-seven years old and still in training at the Jung Institute in Zürich and worried about having enough. She just loved him, and that was that. I remember saying out loud that my brother couldn't do any wrong in her eyes. It felt very depressing to be unable to do something that would get me what I most wanted.

For me, the need for love is at least a bit like the need for alcohol or drugs. In addicts, the need for the addictive substance is so great that they behave without any logic or reason. If one drinks or takes drugs and suffers painful consequences, it is reasonable and logical to quit. If high achievement and all the work and suffering that go with it doesn't produce the love I thought it would, it would seem logical and reasonable for me to stop trying to achieve, or at least back away from striving so intensely that it brought pain and even illness. My early experience in life would say love is likely to come not when I am achieving and strong and reliable and independent but when I am weak, dirty, dependent, and utterly unreliable; but somehow, the need to achieve was like a drug that was so powerful that it overwhelmed logic and reason. It is logical to see the consequences of obsessive achievement as harmful, but logic was overridden by some powerful emotion that wanted something that reason didn't.

While I felt powerless consciously to give up my mad pursuit of achievement, a dream came that I think was trying to help me change, to help me let go of this relentless chasing of achievement to win my mother's love. It occurred just after my open-heart surgery, which followed long years of exhausting overwork. Briefly, the dream was that the *Arc de Triomphe* in Paris had been taken down and replaced by a giant gold bidet. For the French, the *Arc de Triomphe* is a great symbol of all their past victories, successes, and glory, which they display for all the world to see. It is a chest-pounding display of power, reflecting a wish to be the top gun, the best, *le seule*, the nation that stands out among nations. The arch was built in one of the most prominent places in Paris. If you visit Paris, it's hard to miss.

This replacement of the arch with a lowly bidet is a humiliatingly ironic end to a magnificent symbol of power. Because I felt humiliated when I was replaced by my brother, I could imagine the feelings that would be aroused in the French people when they witnessed the substitution of an ordinary bidet for the arch, and I could identify with them. For a Frenchman, such a vile replacement would be a blasphemous besmirching of his nation's honor. It would be the toppling of something of great value and replacing it with something quite lowly. It would make no sense to a Frenchman to replace a great symbol in which he has enormous pride with an ordinary bathroom device that is used to wash the genitals both before and after sex. It is a device kept in the bathroom and used in the dark, in secret, away from public eyes. The dream gives the bidet a place of prominence for all to see. It's the desecration of a thing of beauty and wonder and the apotheosis of something plainly common. From the standpoint of its personal meaning to me, the dream imagery suggests an enormous shift of values is taking place in my unconscious. In the dream, something that once assigned great value to triumph, glory, and honor has been replaced by something that assigns great value to something more humble, lowly, and earthy.

What I can't understand, then, is why, at my age and stage of life, and despite what I felt as a more realistic reordering of values that the arch of triumph dream suggested, I am still feeling an inner pressure to be or at least to appear to be very successful? Wildly unrealistic fantasies are the main source of the pressure. I am still pestered by ludicrously absurd fantasies that have me in possession of stunning houses that, like the dream of Eighteen East 74th Street, show me in possession of something that bespeaks wealth, success, and importance.

In my fantasies, I own splendid residences in Paris and Berlin. I understand a bit why my fantasy would put me in Paris. I've loved Paris for years. It is a special place for me that has appeared often in my dreams. After the *Arc de Triomphe* dream I felt an urge to go live in Paris. That urge is still there and is reflected in my fantasies. The fantasies about Paris and Berlin repeat themselves and seem to portray a long, unsatisfied yearning. At their root, however, I am suspecting that the fantasies about magnificent places to live may be about rediscovering and compensating for the feeling of self-worth I lost as a child when I was ashamed of the shabby condition and appearance of the house I was born into.

Much time and energy go into a powerful fantasy to have a truly breathtaking Paris apartment. I'm talking luxury, eye-popping stuff. I spend hours every day googling apartments for sale in Paris. I spend hours looking through lists. Christie's and Sotheby's carry long lists of the types of apartment that might interest me.

First, I imagine where I'd like to live in Paris. It's not easy to narrow down as there are twenty *arrondissements*, each with its own characteristic pluses and minuses. I think about how important it is to be in a safe neighborhood. Truth is, most of the inner city is relatively safe. Then, I think how nice it would be to be near the Louvre so that I could visit any time and enjoy its incredible collection. *Île Saint-Louis* is also attractive and safe with gorgeous views of Notre Dame. *Île de la Cité* is a great location as well as it lies just between the Marais and the Latin Quarter. Or maybe it would be great to be next to Luxembourg Gardens in order to take long healthy walks and enjoy its beauty. So I started with a survey just to get a general impression. Christie's list has a wide range of choices when it comes to luxury apartments. I'm slowly making my way through the list and see an apartment in the fifth *arrondissement*, the Latin Quarter, that sets off a whole rush of fantasies. It has a roof top garden with a clear view of Notre Dame and the Seine. It has stone and wood walls and old doors and staircases and stone and marble fireplaces. It has an indoor swimming pool hewn from the rock in the basement. Next to the pool is an hammam and a fitness center with treadmills and other sophisticated workout machines. Oh, man. I could just imagine bringing friends and family to see me: Beverly and Mike, Linda and Enrico (they'd be coming from Florence, which, with its magnificent Uffizi Gallery, finishes only second to the Louvre), Phyllis and Kenneth, George and Janine, Peter and Kari, Mel and Patty, and Joyce and Rick, along with my daughters and grandkids. Can you imagine the look on their faces when they enter this place? Oh, man. I get high just thinking about it. There is an extensive wine cellar. So, I think of stocking it with the best French wines, which we'd serve to guests as we sit by the pool. For every day we might have Châteauneuf-du-Pape for red and Pouilly-Fuissé for white, and for special occasions a Rothschild. Nancy and I don't drink, but we love to see the admiring glances of friends when they are offered such a famous and splendid *boisson*.

Of course, our friends would have been quite impressed even before seeing this gorgeous place or drinking our superb wine. I imagine we'd have a subscription to NetJets and would fly them here in a Gulfstream. For a million or so bucks a year we could fly almost as much as we'd like. I find it just as easy and exciting to imagine having a million or so bucks for NetJets as it is to have the money for this apartment, which costs fifteen million dollars. Really, I find it just as easy to imagine fifteen million dollars as it is to imagine one million. So why not? Why hold back when it is all there just for the imagining? I'm feeling wonderful just writing about it. Oh, my! And the moment when our limo picks them up at the airport: of course, we'd meet our friends, and I imagine they'd be gushing about the stewardesses, the service, the plane with its gorgeous appointments, and the limo, and the flight over, and not being able to wait to see the apartment. I get high thinking about it.

Then driving to the apartment there'll be "oohs" and "ahs" as we pass the Eiffel Tower, the *Arc de Triomphe*, Notre Dame, and other famous sights on our way to the Latin Quarter where we live. As we pass the *Arc de Triomphe*, I might share with them my gold bidet dream. That might offend Rick and Joyce a bit, since he is a retired Presbyterian minister and the dream could be seen as a bit irreverent, like one of Jung's dreams of God sitting on a toilet in heaven and dropping a huge turd on the Basel Cathedral. But the dream would not upset Rick as much as they would a patriotic Frenchman, who would see the destruction of the arch and its replacement with a giant douche bowl as an unimaginable act of desecration. On the other hand, Muslims who had immigrated to France might find this desecration of French superiority quite satisfying.

And if you think I am living a fantasy life, which I am, the disparity that I imagine, replacing the *Arc de Triomphe* with a golden bidet, doesn't come close to the disparity of comparing France's former glory with its relatively modest place in today's world. To put that into a personal context, it might be like me still using the title "corporate vice president and officer" of a Fortune 500 company today. Whatever glory that represented, it was a long time ago and will never be regained. When I look at the arch, I am sometimes reminded of the pictures people use in their obituaries. In the photos, they are still twenty-five years old. And their obituaries with the lists of all their achievements are as far from the complete truth about them as the *Arc de Triomphe* is from France's present reality. That dream of the arch was a big one, and at the time I was very tempted to quit my job and go to Paris. I felt the dream tugging on me to go there and explore the meaning of such a strange but dramatic dream. But my practical self won, and I stayed on in my job for a few years more.

We'd also pass by the *Île de la Cité*. I'd be tempted to mention a very dramatic incident that occurred to me there. When I was there in 1986, the central police station was on the *Île de la Cité*. One morning I was going there to apply for a visa with the hope of remaining in France for two years. As I left my apartment that morning, a friend told me to be careful. For several weeks, there had been terrorist bombings all around Paris, in restaurants, department stores, and movies. A Lebanese terrorist had shot and killed the Israeli ambassador to France. The French had caught and imprisoned several Lebanese for the crime. As a result, other terrorists came to France and began a bombing campaign to force the French government to release the terrorists. As I left, I said to my friend that I was going to the central police station, probably the safest place in Paris. As I stood in the visa line, which was in the basement of the police headquarters, there was suddenly a deafening explosion about thirty feet from where I was standing. It killed and injured many people. There were corpses and fingers and other limbs scattered around me. Through an astonishing piece of luck, I had been standing in line at a point that was behind one of the big floor-to-ceiling columns. With the column's protection, the force of the blast completely missed me. But it was a terrifying moment, and ambulances were carrying people away for hours. The incident scared me so much that I left Paris very soon thereafter and returned to the states. When I got back to the states, I had a letter from the lady who rented me my small apartment in the Fifteenth. She said she had found something of mine left behind and had put it in the mail. She also mentioned that the bombing stopped almost as soon as I left. She added: *quelle coincidence.* She had a very nice sense of humor. I was disappointed that I didn't feel safe staying longer in Paris.

I had come there from Zürich, where I had been studying at the C.G. Jung Institute to become a Jungian analyst. I had been in Zürich for four years after a midlife career change which was to transform me from corporate executive to student and, I hoped, to psychoanalyst. After four years in Zürich, however, I had made little progress toward my goal and had not even been able to prepare to take the propadeuticum, which is an exam one has to pass before going on to the final clinical work and exams. After about a year in Zürich, I had fallen into a deep depression that lasted for two years. I felt like an utter failure. I had entered this new phase of my life with such forward-looking zeal and big plans for the future. All that had simply fizzled out. Part of the problem was my analysis. For the first year in Zürich, I had a very good one, but my analyst had to leave to go to Canada. Then I unwisely chose an analyst who, despite his encyclopedic knowledge of Jung, was a practicing alcoholic. It took me a while to discover that, while our chemistry became increasingly toxic. I began to lose interest in everything except the idea of going to Paris to try to write. It felt to me that I needed to write something about my dream of the bidet and the *Arc de Triomphe*. The wish to do that had gnawed at me ever since I said "no" to going to Paris immediately after I had the dream. I felt a kind of suspended animation about the dream and its meaning. So, after a few months of struggle, I decided to move to Paris. But Paris didn't take this time, either. Fate intervened with a bomb, which caused me to leave Paris and left me with a yearning to return that has become a kind of permanent resident in my psyche and my imagination. My mind just won't let go of Paris and the possibility of a glorious life there.

I'm thinking of this as, in my fantasy, we drive toward our fifteen-million-dollar dream apartment. After this kind of circuitous journey, past various Paris monuments and places of interest, we finally arrive at our apartment. I imagine our friends' faces as they walk into this wondrous place. We show them their rooms and give them time to tidy up before we give them the grand tour. I imagine some of them wanting to go for a swim or have a sauna right away in order to refresh themselves from their long flight. We take our time for all this and then meet at the pool before dinner for drinks and hors d'oeuvres. Afterwards, I imagine taking them to *Tour d'Argent* for dinner of duck in all its splendor. They say you rarely see a real French person at *La Tour d'Argent*. It's a show for tourists, and a fabulous, four-star Michelin meal can be had at other places for much less. But it's an unimaginably artistic show that the folks at *La Tour d'Argent* put on. Nancy and I had been there before, so I imagine us spending the evening watching our friends' faces and the animated and approving reactions to the brilliant display, after which we'd catch the show at *Folies Bergère*. I'm not sure how Rick and Joyce will react to this blatant display of nakedness but, who knows, maybe they'll get a kick out of it. Rick and Joyce have definitely relaxed their perspectives a bit since leaving the active ministry.

I must also add, a bit immodestly, that my German is even better than my French. So, why stop at Paris? I need someplace to impress friends with my German and my fancy house in Berlin. I was fluent in German when I left Zürich, and I probably would regain my fluency with just a little time, effort, and exposure. My learning German is another example of my need for love and the price I will pay to earn it.

In my fantasies, I've found a great house in Berlin. I went through lists of apartments and houses for sale in Berlin the way I had for Paris when I imagined moving there. The beautiful house I found only costs three and a half million dollars. For what you get, Berlin is far less expensive than Paris. It's at the foot of the *Kurfürstendamm* on the Halensee. All rooms in the house have a view of the lake. *Kurfürstendamm* is the *Champs Elysées* of Berlin, with its many restaurants and cafes, fine boutiques such as Gucci, Louis Vuitton, Chanel, and Cartier, hip designer shops and art galleries. I am drawn to Berlin not only because of an urge to show off my fluent

German and impressive digs, but also, and hopefully more importantly, because of the powerful dream about Jesus and "*Ich Bin Ein Berliner*" that I discussed earlier, which made me feel such a strong psychic connection with Berlin. I hate to admit this, but I came to think that the Berliner dream meant, among other things, that God, the Self, wanted me to end up in Berlin, to reach home finally, even if it is as far away from my actual home as my psychological home is from my ego. I have to keep reminding myself that "home" keeps changing, so that we are there only provisionally and momentarily before it changes again. In the end, there is no "finally."

Recently, I have become aware that my dreams and fantasies about magnificent houses and apartments, like those in Paris and Berlin, likely compensate the deep shame I felt growing up in my house in Oklahoma. It had fallen into such disrepair and neglect that it embarrassed the entire family, so much so that we never invited anyone other than family members into our house. I suspect this experience early in life caused me to resolve later in life to own residences that were attractive and bespoke a successful person of worth.

Shame is a very interesting feeling that affects us powerfully. While it feels a lot like guilt, it is different. Guilt stems from a feeling that I have done something bad, that I have broken some rule or law; shame comes from a feeling that I am intrinsically bad, that I am unworthy.

As I thought about this recently, I wondered why a child would blame himself for the condition of his house, as if he felt responsible for the house and the burden of shame that went with it? Why wouldn't he blame his parents, or fate, or God for delivering him into such a family? I can only conclude we are somehow wired to feel that way. However, I can also imagine that taking such responsibility gives the child an unconscious sense of power to compensate his conscious feelings of powerlessness and helplessness. Perhaps, it is an unconscious identification with God that leads him later to the psychological and spiritual need to separate, to disidentify himself from God in order to find God. These are speculations at best, but they have a ring of truth to them. I also suspect that the shame I felt about my house led me to do all I could do to be successful enough to live in houses in which I would never again feel that shame.

Shame causes my fantasies about owning grand places like Eighteen East 74th Street and luxurious Paris and Berlin residences. It even leads to fantasies of winning the lottery in order to have sufficient funds to buy them. My feeling of responsibility as a child for the shameful condition of my house leads me to the suspicion that my feeling of responsibility for who I am may be equally misplaced. It may be God, not I, who is responsible for who I am, just as it certainly was God who was responsible for the house, the parents, the country, the state and the town I was dropped into as a child.

While I was born and live now in America, in a small town in Oklahoma where I was born, some five thousand miles away from Berlin, as a result of my "*Ich Bin Ein Berliner*" dream, in my heart and soul, I feel Berlin is home. This, perhaps, is a somewhat more respectable and less shallow reason for wanting to have a home in Berlin than its closeness to the Kurfürstendamm and my shallow fantasies of wishing to impress friends with my German, wealth, intelligence, and importance. While my mind is ashamed of these shallow fantasies, my emotions, shaped long ago by my mother and embedded in me, will not let go of them. Nor am I entirely willing to knock these fantasies, shallow as they may be. Fantasies add to what we are in wonderful ways that have led me to conclude that reality is okay only if that is the best you can do. Our fantasies can make us much bigger, more interesting, and more wonderous than we otherwise might be.

One of the possible rewards of becoming like a child again may be the birth of an imaginary state in which we regain our feelings of grandiosity and the uninhibited and unfiltered expression of them that is undiminished by their apparent absurdity. Feeling great may actually be much more pleasant than just being considered great. The imposter syndrome may well keep us from feeling great even when we have achieved it in the eyes of others. Hemingway may have suffered this fate. Is it possible that the imagined world of greatness of a child is preferable to actual greatness devoid of the feeling? Which state is closer to the kingdom of heaven? If one is in heaven and doesn't feel it, is one really there? And what feeling might we have imagining ourselves sitting next to God? Is it love, or acceptance, or greatness, or specialness? Or is it all of these? A child can embrace feelings that aren't supported by reality. It is often more difficult for an adult.

I'm coming to the view that achievement and the love, recognition, and acceptance that go with it may have no intrinsic value. These things may be valuable only because we are wired to believe so. They are the Self's creative tools that serve to ignite and sustain creation. They are what paint brushes and clay and musical notes are to artists. And the Self has a very creative way of making sure its tools are used. I am remembering a conversation with a client, where I asked him what he thought he would have to do for his mother to love him. His reply was, "I would have to become Jesus." Now that would be quite an achievement. His comment made me think later that the profound need for mother's love and our failure to get enough of it leads to a lifelong endless effort to achieve that which will cause her to love us, even long after she is dead.

Very early, when we are infants, the Self makes sure mother, no matter how good or bad she may later become, gives us a free sample of the love potion. Mother gives us that look of unconditional love. There is no price to pay. It is free. We didn't have to do or achieve anything. In the case of humans, the free sample got us hooked for life. We loved that free sample so much that later, when we had to pay for it, when mother and others made us earn the love and recognition and acceptance we received, we would do almost anything to get some more of it. The earned love gave us the potion in a diluted form. It still felt good, but never good enough to satisfy us. So, we spent our lives unsatisfied, or if we were, satisfied only for brief moments, as in the case of an orgasm. But we kept trying to get back to that incomparable early feeling of "that look" from momma. We wanted that buzz again. We kept trying to achieve, hoping beyond hope that we would get back to the mother lode. But we couldn't get back, because the Self didn't want us to get back. Creation would have stopped. This was

Goethe's message when he said that divine discontent drives us incessantly into and accounts for all creative production.

I suppose that, to make this point, I could have suggested that you just read Goethe, but that wouldn't have helped my own process of self-discovery the way that writing this book has. The writing has followed its own path, twists and turns that were hard to stay with at times. I've worked through regrets and failings, disappointments and triumphs. Now the end of all of this self-exploration is finally coming into focus. As I see it, the purpose of this book, of the whole writing process, is to show me who I am.

In that process, I have become aware of two opposites that exist side by side inside me, my real world and its opposite, my imagined world. I sit in the tiny crack between them. I'm the bridge that connects them. The world I imagine inside me seems just as real as the actual real world outside me. Still, my mind knows the difference between the two. I am also aware that my imagined world sometimes, but by no means always, actually becomes real. Like an architect, some, but not all, of the plans and ideas hatched inside himself become buildings outside himself. But many don't. That's the way the creative process works. My movement between these two worlds, from imagined to real and back, is a picture of the creative process. Who I am and who I am becoming is a reflection of that process.

I've come to think that the essence of who I am is captured in the phrase, *Ich Bin Ein Berliner*, because to be a Berliner is to be a reflection of the creative process that is the mystery that unfolds in us all, just as it did for Berlin. This unfolding may survive our physical death and persist into eternity. There is hard evidence that energy is never lost; it just transforms into something else. It's a process that turns us into who we are and who we are becoming, and also turns everything else into what it is. In this sense, we are all Berliners. And to be a true Berliner we also have to at least try to tear down the inner wall that creates a gap that separates us from the other side of our psychic city. I think I've made some holes in the wall through which many strangers from the other side have slipped. But my entire wall is not yet down. I'm still working on it, and I feel as though I am doing this work in an inner Berlin, even though I am not physically there.

Life, however, is a motion picture; not a snapshot. This book is based on my life. But the minute I put down my pen I am left with a snapshot of who I am; however, the motion picture, my life, continues. And as my life continues, who I am continues to expand. So it is unlikely we can ever capture who we are entirely. We just do the best we can.

Knowing who I am becoming still leaves unanswered the question of who or what is the author of my unfolding, the architect of the person I am becoming. Am I the helpless victim of the creative Self? Am I the beneficiary — unworthy and undeserving though I might be — of the creative Self? Or am I both? I suspect that I am both victim and beneficiary of the creative Self, its casualty and the recipient of its largesse.

As I have been thinking back over my life, I recently read the book, *A Matter of Death and Life,* by Marilyn and Irvin Yalom. They both say, looking back upon their lives, that they would change nothing. He believes he and his wife have lived a regret-free life and that that is the only way to avoid the dread of death. I agree with the Yaloms in that I also would change nothing, but probably for different reasons. I wouldn't change anything, not because everything was so wonderful and free of regret, but because the change would make me someone other than who I am. I have many regrets, but for the same reason would not, even if the opportunity were afforded me, change anything I did to cause the things I now regret.

Given my age and health, death must be waiting nearby. I'm unaware of any terror or dread. Dying is one of the few things in my life that feels normal. I suspect that years of meditation, in my case, have protected me against the dread of death. I have a very strong feeling that when I transcend in meditation, when I lose the mantra and enter momentarily another state of consciousness, that I have already, quite briefly but time and again, experienced death. And that transcendent state is far from a dreadful one. It feels like going to my inner Berlin. It is, in fact, pleasant and desirable. I think in the East people may have discovered something that makes it easier to face and accept death. Of course, I won't know for sure until the time comes.

My dreams and my writing have shown me that Berlin may indeed be the only place where both my physical and psychic self feel completely at home, side by side. So, if I do go to Berlin, it will be to die there.

References

Eliade, M. (1987). *The Sacred and The Profane: The Nature of Religion*. Harcourt Brace Jovanovich.

Frost, R.(1914). *North of Boston*. Henry Holt & Company.

Goethe, J. (1949). *Truth and Fantasy From My Life*. (J. Cohen, Ed.). Indiana University.

Hesse, H. (2002). *Steppenwolf: a Novel*. Henry Holt and Company. (Original work published 1927)

Jung, C. (1973). *The Symbolic Life: Miscellaneous Writings*. Princeton University Press. (Original work published 1953)

Jung, C. (1974). *Psychological Types*. Princeton University Press. (Original work published 1954)

Jung, C. (1976). *Symbols of Transformation*. Princeton University Press. (Original work published 1956)

Jung, C. & W., W. (1961, January 23). *The Bill W. – Carl Jung Letters*. [Correspondence]. The AA Grapevine, Inc., North Hollywood, CA. https://silkworth.net/

wp-content/uploads/2020/07/The-Bill-W-Carl-Jung-Letters-Jan-1963.pdf

King James Bible. (2021). King James Bible Online. https://www.kingjamesbibleonline.org/

Layard, J. (1977). *The Virgin Archetype: The Incest Taboo and The Virgin Archetype / On Psychic Consciousness.* Spring Publications.

Paine, T. (2016). *Common Sense: The Origin and Design of Government.* Coventry House Publishing. (Original work published 1776)

Proust, M. (2003). *Time Regained: In Search of Lost Time* (Vol. 6) (A. Mayor & T. Kilmartin, Trans.). Modern Library. (Original work published 1925)

Winnicott, D. (1971). *Playing and Reality.* Tavistock/Routledge.

Wirt, W. (2017). *Life and Character of Patrick Henry.* Andesite Press. (Original work published 1817)

Yalom, I. & Yalom, M. (2021). *A Matter of Death and Life.* Stanford University Press.

Lightning Source UK Ltd.
Milton Keynes UK
UKHW021017230822
407709UK00001BA/127